CLASSIC SERMONS
ON THE
APOSTLE PAUL

KREGEL CLASSIC SERMONS Series

KREGEL CLASSIC SERMONS SERIES

CLASSIC SERMONS ON THE APOSTLE PAUL

Compiled by
Warren W. Wiersbe

kregel
PUBLICATIONS

Grand Rapids, MI 49501

Classic Sermons on the Apostle Paul
Compiled by Warren W. Wiersbe

Published by Kregel Publications, a division of Kregel, Inc.,
P.O. Box 2607, Grand Rapids, MI 49501. Kregel Publications provides trusted, biblical publications for Christian
growth and service. Your comments and suggestions are
valued.

Cover painting: *The Apostle Paul* by Rembrandt, c. 1635,
     Kunsthistorifchet Museum, Vienna
Cover and book design: Alan G. Hartman

Library of Congress Cataloging-in-Publication Data

Classic sermons on the apostle Paul / [compiled by] Warren
W. Wiersbe.
       p.   cm.— (Kregel classic sermons series)
     Includes index.
     1. Paul, the Apostle, Saint—Sermons. 2. Sermons,
American. 3. Sermons, English. I. Wiersbe, Warren W.
II. Series: Kregel classic sermons series.
BS2506.C54   1996   225.9'2—dc20   96-10311
                                                                CIP

ISBN   0-8254-4075-0

Printed in the United States of America
1 2 3 4 5 / 00 99 98 97 96

CONTENTS

LIST OF SCRIPTURE TEXTS

PREFACE

THE *KREGEL CLASSIC SERMONS SERIES* is an attempt to assemble and publish meaningful sermons from master preachers about significant themes.

These are *sermons*, not essays or chapters taken from books about themes. Not all of these sermons could be called great, but all of them are *meaningful*. They apply the truths of the Bible to the needs of the human heart, which is something that all effective preaching must do.

While some are better known than others, all of the preachers whose sermons I have selected had important ministries and were highly respected in their day. The fact that a sermon is included in this volume does not mean that either the compiler or the publisher agrees with or endorses everything that the man did, preached, or wrote. The sermon is here because it has a valued contribution to make.

These are sermons about *significant* themes. The pulpit is no place to play with trivia. The preacher has thirty minutes in which to help mend broken hearts, change defeated lives, and save lost souls; he can never accomplish this demanding ministry by distributing homiletical tidbits. In these difficult days we do not need clever pulpiteers who discuss the times; we need dedicated ambassadors who will preach the eternities.

The reading of these sermons can enrich your spiritual life. The studying of them can enrich your skills as an interpreter and expounder of God's truth. However God uses these sermons in your life and ministry, my prayer is that His church around the world will be encouraged and strengthened by them.

WARREN W. WIERSBE

Paul

Clarence Edward Macartney (1879–1957) ministered
in Paterson, New Jersey, and Philadelphia, Pennsylvania,
before assuming the influential pastorate of First
Presbyterian Church, Pittsburgh, Pennsylvania, where
he ministered for twenty-seven years. His preaching
especially attracted men, not only to the Sunday
services but also to his popular Tuesday noon luncheons.
He was gifted in dealing with Bible biographies and, in
this respect, has been called "the American Alexander
Whyte." Much of his preaching was topical-textual, but
it was always biblical, doctrinal, and practical. Perhaps
his most famous sermon is "Come Before Winter."

The sermon I have selected is taken from *He Chose
Twelve*, reprinted in 1993 by Kregel Publications.

Clarence Edward Macartney

1

PAUL

ON A MARCH AFTERNOON in the year of salvation A.D. 60, a gang of prisoners under the custody of a Roman centurion is descending the western slope of the Alban Hills. Each prisoner is chained to a soldier. This one is a man-stealer from Alexandria, this one a robber from Tyre, this one a murderer from Caesarea, this one a rebel from Jerusalem. All look the part save this last prisoner, who is a Hebrew who has appealed to the jurisdiction of Caesar and is being taken to Rome to stand before Caesar's judgment seat.

The Appian Way leads them across the vast spaces of the Roman campaign, now brilliant with the flowers of springtime. Now they are passing over the plain that, at a day not far distant, will be honeycombed with narrow subterranean passages where men will lay their dead in hope of the doctrine of the resurrection that fell from the lips of the Jewish prisoner. As they come nearer to the city, the road is filled with throngs of people coming and going—farmers returning with empty carts from the market; cohorts of soldiers starting for the distant east or coming home after service in Africa, Greece, or Asia; wealthy men, carried in litters by slaves, on their way to their summer villas on the hills, the chariots of generals and senators and proconsuls.

To Julius and his band of prisoners all these give hardly a glance as they pass. Now the prisoners pass by the colossal tombs of the great men of Rome, then at length into the city, past temples, statues, arches, baths, colonnades, and palaces whose gilded roofs flash back the afternoon sun down into the Forum and up the Capitoline Hill to the barracks of the praetorian guard, where Julius hands over his prisoners.

The dream of one of these prisoners has come true! He has come to Rome! Yet, save among a few obscure believers, his entry excited not a ripple of interest or comment. Rome's greatest conqueror entered her gates that day. When the proud monuments of imperial splendor upon which this prisoner gazed as he passed through the city shall have been leveled with the dust and under the dust, Rome's most conspicuous monument will be a temple dedicated to the faith of that lonely prisoner.

It is not my purpose to speak of Paul's place in history. That place is forever secure. As one of the inspired texts of history, Saint Paul needs no explanation and no defense. What I wish to do rather is to say something of the man who did these mighty works, the messenger who carried the message that turned the world upside down, the lamp that bore the light that lighted the darkness of this world.

Paul once asked the Corinthians to be followers of him as he was of Christ. Who could imitate Paul—the versatility of his genius, his great experience with Christ, the power and cogency of his thought, and the eloquence of his tongue? Yet there is much in him that is capable of imitation and where humble Christians can follow him. Of that let us now speak.

His Self-Image

First, his appreciation of the dignity of human nature. This is always a mark of a great soul. Paul showed his high thought of the worth and dignity of man by a high regard for himself. I have always counted it a fortunate thing that he who is the great teacher as to the sinfulness of man and the corruption of human nature was no mealymouthed weakling, but the manliest man who ever lived. We have an instance of this in Paul's reply to the Roman officers at Philippi, who, when they discovered that they had scourged and imprisoned without trial a Roman citizen, sent down messengers asking Paul to withdraw quietly from the city. But Paul answered in all the splendor of his self-respect, "They have beaten us openly uncondemned, being Romans, and have cast us into prison; and now they thrust us out privily? Nay, verily; but let them come themselves and fetch us out" (Acts 16:37). We have another echo of this in his rebuke of the high priest who, at the trial of Paul before the Sanhedrin, commanded the soldier to smite Paul on the mouth. Instantly Paul scorched him with the flame of his righteous indignation: "God shall smite thee, thou whited wall: for sittest thou to judge me after the law, and commandest me to be smitten contrary to the law?" (Acts 23:3). It was a ringing testimony to the rights of man. Paul was able to respect himself because, he tells us, he always lived so as to have a conscience void of offense toward God and man. If Paul was a chosen vessel, let it be remembered that he was also a clean vessel before he was chosen. The first factor in any good and useful life is the respect of self. The man who does not live so as to have his own self-respect cannot hope to reach or touch other men.

Self-knowledge, self-reverence, self-control—
These three alone lead life to sovereign power.

A Man for All

Second, his love for others. He who had such high thoughts of the worth and dignity of human nature was a fit vessel to bear to the world the doctrines of the Gospel which affirmed the worth of every soul and a noble destiny through faith in Christ. Yet this love for others was not a natural gift with Paul. Of all men, at the outset, he would seem the least qualified to become the bearer of the tidings that God had made of one blood all nations of men. He appears in the theater of human action as a man possessed by the fiercest prejudices and antipathies, as an intense nationalist of the straightest sect, seeing nothing good beyond the confines of Israel. Yet this man, through the touch of Christ, becomes the apostle to the Gentiles, the first preacher of the doctrine of a nation of humanity, which is above all other nations. His traveling band, made up

of Timothy, half Greek and half Hebrew, Luke the
Greek, Aristarchus and Sopater who were Macedonians,
and Trophimus who was an Asiatic, was the first society of internationalists the world had ever seen.

When Paul died, his arms were stretched as wide
apart as those of Christ upon the cross. In Chrysostom's
eloquent words, "The dust of that heart which a man
would not do wrong to call the heart of the world, so
enlarged that it could take in cities, and nations, and
peoples." The "desperate tides" of the whole world's
anguish was forced through the channels of a single
heart "Who is weak, and I am not weak? Who is made
to stumble, and I burn not?" (2 Cor. 11:29 RV). He was
debtor to all men, all races, all classes, all colors. Wherever a man breathed, wherever a heart beat, wherever
a soul was enshrined, there was Paul with all his burning earnestness and yearning love.

He was able to think nothing alien to himself. When
John Howard, the prisoner-reformer, died in a Russian
lazzaretto, they put on his grave these words: "Reader,
whosoever thou art, know that thou standest by the
grave of a friend." Did we know where rests the dust of
Paul, we could write like words over his tomb: "Reader,
whosoever thou art, bond or free, Greek or barbarian,
Jew or Gentile, black or white, red or yellow, man of
the first, fifteenth, or twentieth century, know that
thou standest by the grave of a friend."

A Man Born for Adversity

Third, the heroic element in the life of Paul. In our
day there is a tendency to think that the heroism of
the Christian life is to be found apart from great Christian beliefs and convictions. It is, therefore, a fact worthy of pause and reflection that it is the man of the
deepest and most clearly outlined beliefs and doctrines
who is also the noblest of the Christian heroes, as Chrysostom called him, "the wrestler for Christ."

In his libelous *Life of St. Paul*, Renan, meaning to
contrast Paul unfavorably with Jesus, says: "To appear
for a moment, to reflect a soft and profound refulgence,

to die very young, is the life of a God. To struggle, dispute and conquer is the life of a man." Not in the disparaging sense in which Renan meant it, to struggle, dispute and, sometimes, to conquer, is the life of a man. We do not know a man until we have seen how he performs on the lonely platform of adversity, how he will act with the wind in his face. If there was ever a man born for adversity and who inspires his fellowmen to take arms against a sea of troubles and by opposing end them, that man was Saint Paul. It was no rhetoric, no mere figure of speech, when he spoke of bearing in his body the marks of the Lord Jesus Christ.

What a catalog of woes he mentions—thorns in the flesh and sicknesses of the body; through adversaries of the civil government, beatings and imprisonment; the frenzy of the mobs who stoned him and clamored for his blood; the oath-bound assassins who dogged his tracks; the perils of the natural world by sea, by river, in wilderness, and on mountaintop; the desertion and suspicion of his friends; cruel slander which, like a viper, has rustled in the withered leaves of dry and fallen hearts since the world began.

Heroic battler, noble wrestler for Christ! How many were your adversaries! Was there a peril of sky or earth or sea that he did not face? Was there a wicked passion in the heart of man that did not select him for its victim? Was there a cup of bitterness that he did not taste? Was there a thorn to which the flesh is heir that he did not endure? Yet in all things he was more than conqueror.

It is here that all of us become deeply interested in Paul. We all must face life, and if it can be done triumphantly, we want to know how. In Paul's triumph there were at least three elements:

His aim and purposes did not end with self. If his own pleasure and comfort and personal success had been his aim, then what a bitter disappointment life must have been to Paul! But he had scorn for those miserable aims that end with self. Personal defeats and overthrows did not shake his soul. Those personal vicissitudes which shock and overcome so many men were but minor incidents to this man whose mind was set on a higher goal than self.

God had a purpose to work out in his life. Whatever, therefore, the hard experience through which he had to pass, he could look under it and beyond it and back of it to the will and purpose of God. Things did not "happen" to Paul. The man who gives us the sublime and difficult doctrine about the sovereign decree of almighty God is also the man who gives us the incomparable demonstration of how that faith works in everyday life. He not only said it, but found it to be true, that sentence imbedded like a lovely crystal in the dark rock of the great chapter on predestination, "All things work together for good to them that love God" (Rom. 8:26).

His fellowship with Christ was so close that he could make bold to say that Christ suffered in him. Scotland has given many martyrs to the church and to civil liberty, but there is no tale of martyrdom that so touches a Scottish heart as that of the two Wigtown martyrs, Mary and Agnes Wilson, who perished in the Solway tide. The elder sister was fastened to a stake much farther out than the younger, with the thought that when the younger saw the sufferings and death struggles of her sister she would recant. Quickly the inexorable tide of the Solway came in, first to the ankles, then to the knees, then to the waist, then to the neck, then to the lips. The executioners called to the younger sister, "Look! What seest thou?" Turning her head a little she saw the struggles of her drowning sister and then made her calm answer, "What do I see? I see the Lord Jesus suffering in one of His members!" In the darkest and most critical hours of his life Saint Paul was conscious of the presence and the help of Christ— "But the Lord stood by me" (2 Tim. 4:17 RV).

A Man of Affection

Paul's was a heart that burned for everyone who was lost and was broken down by a brother's tears.

Even if we did not have so many recorded instances of the deeply affectionate nature of Saint Paul, we should know him to be that sort of man, for back of every great and good and lasting work there beats somewhere a warm and tender heart. Napoleon at St. Helena wondered if in all the world a single person loved him. But to do justice to the friendships of Saint Paul would require the tongue not of man, but of an angel. In his letters come first the doctrines, then the practical precepts, and last the personal greetings to Onesiphorus, who was not ashamed of his chains; to Epaphroditus, who came to minister to him in Rome and whom Paul nursed back to life; to Amplias, Narcissus, Herodian, Julia, Olympas, Rufus and "his mother and mine"; and then that last urgent message for best-loved Timothy to come "before winter."

He who could smite with a Titan's fist the stronghold of Satan knew also how to lay a forget-me-not on the breast of a living friend or upon the grave of the dead. The thought of those friends whom he had made for himself and for Christ, "hearts he had won of sister or of brother, friends in the blameless family of God," the thought of these friends, the remembrance that they prayed for him, came like gleams of sunlight into the damp and gloom of that Mamertine dungeon at Rome. Salute! Salute! Salute! is his word as they lead him out to die. And thus with messages for those whose names he had written in the Lamb's Book of Life, Paul fades from this world into that other world where friends meet and forever are fair and where partings are no more.

All these friendships were summed up in the great and eternal friendship with Christ. That is why Paul's life is the greatest love story ever written. Love carried him over the blazing plains and miasmic marshes; love led him through the ghettos of the great Roman cities; love was the star by which he steered his course through the stormy Aegean and Mediterranean. If I were asked to sum up his theology, his doctrine, I would not mention his great fundamental teachings as to the fall of man and the sinfulness that requires redemption; nor his profound statement as to the sovereign purposes of God's grace; nor his logical setting forth of the doctrine of justification by faith. I would sum it up in one single sentence, that sentence which must sum up all genuine Christianity, all true saving relationship with Christ: "I live by the faith of the Son of God, who loved me, and gave himself for me." That mighty life is but the echo of that sentence which takes in the length and the depth and the breadth and the height of our faith, He "loved me, and gave himself for me." Forever true! As true of you as it was of Paul or John. Christ loved you and gave Himself for you. But have you consented to that fact? Have you bowed down before it? Can you say it as Paul said it, He loved me and gave Himself for me?

> Christ! I am Christ's, and let the name suffice you,
> Yea, for me too He greatly hath sufficed;
> Lo, with no winning word I would entice you,
> Paul has no honor and no friend but Christ!

NOTES

Saul's Conversion

George Whitefield (1714–1770) was born in
Gloucester, England, and educated at Pembroke
College, Oxford. There he came under the influence of
John Wesley and Charles Wesley, although Whitefield
was more Calvinistic in doctrine than they. Ordained
in the Anglican Church, he quickly gained a reputation
as an effective preacher, but the Anglican churches
disapproved of him because of his association with the
Methodists. He began to preach to great crowds out of
doors and led John Wesley to follow his example.

Whitefield made seven visits to America and is
recognized as one of the leaders of evangelism and
spiritual awakening in American history. This sermon
is taken from *Memoirs of George Whitefield*, edited by
John Gilles and published in 1837 by Hunt and Noyes.

George Whitefield

2

SAUL'S CONVERSION

But Saul increased the more in strength, and confounded
the Jews which dwelt at Damascus, proving that this is
very Christ (Acts 9:22).

IT IS AN UNDOUBTED truth, however it may seem a
paradox to natural men, that "all that will live godly in
Christ Jesus shall suffer persecution" (2 Tim. 3:12).
And therefore it is very remarkable that our blessed
Lord, in His glorious Sermon on the Mount, after He
had been pronouncing those blessed who were in spirit
meek, pure in heart, and such like, immediately adds
(and spends no less than three verses in this beatitude),
"Blessed are they which are persecuted for
righteousness' sake" (Matt. 5:10). No one ever was or
ever will be endowed with the aforementioned graces
in any degree but he will be persecuted for it in a
measure. There is an irreconcilable enmity between
the seed of the woman and the seed of the serpent.
And if we are not of the world, but show by our fruits
that we are of the number of those whom Jesus Christ
has chosen out of the world, for that very reason the
world will hate us. As this is true of every particular
Christian, so it is true of every Christian church in
general. For some years past we have heard but little
of a public persecution. Why? Because but little of the
power of godliness has prevailed among all
denominations. The strong man armed has had full
possession of most professors' hearts, and therefore he
has let them rest in a false peace. But we may assure
ourselves, when Jesus Christ begins to gather in His
elect in any remarkable manner and opens an effectual
door for preaching the everlasting Gospel, persecution
will flame out, and Satan and his emissaries will do

their utmost (though all in vain) to stop the work of God. Thus it was in the first ages, thus it is in our days, and thus it will be until time shall be no more.

Christians and Christian churches must then expect enemies. Our chief concern should be to learn how to behave toward them in a Christian manner. For unless we take good heed to ourselves, we shall embitter our spirits and act in a manner unbecoming the followers of that Lord "who, when he was reviled, reviled not again; when he suffered, he threatened not" (1 Peter 2:23), and, as a lamb before his shearers is dumb, "so opened he not his mouth" (Acts 8:32). But what motive shall we make use of to bring ourselves to this blessed lamblike temper? Next to the immediate operation of the Holy Spirit upon our hearts, I know of no consideration more conducive to teach us long-suffering toward our most bitter persecutors than this, "That, for all that we know to the contrary, some of those very persons, who are now persecuting, may be chosen from all eternity by God, and hereafter called in time, to edify and build up the church of Christ."

The persecutor Saul, mentioned in the words of the text, (and whose conversion, God willing, I propose to treat of in the following discourse) is a noble instance of this kind.

I say, a persecutor, and that a bloody one. See how he is introduced in the beginning of this chapter: "And Saul, yet breathing out threatenings and slaughter against the disciples of the Lord, went unto the high priest, and desired of him letters to Damascus to the synagogues, that if he found any of this way, whether they were men or women, he might bring them bound to Jerusalem" (9:1–2).

"And Saul, yet breathing out." This implies that he had been a persecutor before. To prove which, we need only look back to the seventh chapter where we shall find him so very remarkably active at Stephen's death, that "the witnesses laid down their clothes at a young man's feet, whose name was Saul" (7:58). He seems, though young, to be in some authority.

Perhaps, for his zeal against the Christians, he was preferred in the synagogue and was allowed to sit in the great council or Sanhedrim. We are told in chapter 8, verse 1, that "Saul was consenting unto his death"; and again, in verse 3, he is brought in as exceeding all in his opposition, for thus speaks the evangelist, "As for Saul, he made havock of the church, entering into every house, and haling men and women committed them to prison." One would have imagined that this should have satisfied, at least abated, the fury of this young zealot. No! Being exceedingly mad against them, as he himself informs Agrippa, and having made havoc of all in Jerusalem, he now is resolved to persecute the disciples of the Lord even to strange cities and therefore is yet breathing out threatening.

"Breathing out." The words are very emphatical and expressive of his bitter enmity. It was as natural to him now to threaten the Christians as it was for him to breathe; he could scarcely speak but it was some threatenings against them. No, he not only breathed out threatenings, but slaughter also (and those who threaten would also slaughter if it were in their power)· against the disciples of the Lord. Insatiable therefore as hell, finding he could not refute or stop the Christians by force of argument, he is resolved to do it by force of arms. Therefore he went to the high priest (for there never was a persecution yet without a high priest at the head of it) and desired of him letters, issued out of his spiritual court, to the synagogues or ecclesiastical courts at Damascus, giving him authority "that if he found any of this way, whether they were men or women, he might bring them bound unto Jerusalem" (9:2), I suppose to be arraigned and condemned in the high priest's court. Observe how he speaks of the Christians. Luke, who wrote the Acts, calls them disciples of the Lord, and Saul styles them men and women of *this way*. I doubt not but he represented them as a company of upstart enthusiasts that had lately gotten into a new method or way of living that would not be content with the temple service, but they must be righteous overmuch and have their private meetings or conventicles and break bread, as they called it, from house to house, to the great disturbance of the established clergy and to the utter subversion of all order and decency. I do not hear that the high priest makes any objection. No, he was as willing to grant letters as Saul was to ask them and wonderfully pleased within himself to find he had such an active zealot to employ against the Christians.

Well then, a judicial process is immediately issued out with the high priest's seal affixed to it. And now I think I see the young persecutor finely equipped and pleasing himself with thoughts how triumphantly he should ride back with men and women of this way dragging after him to Jerusalem.

What a condition may we imagine the poor disciples at Damascus were in at this time! No doubt they had heard of Saul's imprisoning and making havoc of the saints at Jerusalem and we may well suppose were apprised of his design against them. I am persuaded this was a growing, because a trying, time with these dear people. O how did they wrestle with God in prayer, beseeching Him either to deliver them from or give them grace sufficient to enable them to bear up under the fury of their persecutors? The high priest doubtless with the rest of his reverend brethren flattered themselves that they waited with impatience for Saul's return.

But He that sitteth in heaven laughs them to scorn, the Lord has them in derision (see Ps. 2:4). And therefore, verse 3. As Saul journeyed and came even near to Damascus, perhaps to the very gates (our Lord permitting this to try the faith of His disciples and, more conspicuously, to baffle the designs of His enemies), "suddenly [at midday, as he acquaints Agrippa] there shined round about him a light from heaven" (Acts 9:3), a light brighter than the sun, "and he fell to the earth [why not into hell?], and heard a voice saying unto him, Saul, Saul, why persecutest thou me?" (v. 4). The word is doubled, Saul, Saul, like that of our Lord to Martha; Martha, Martha; or the prophet, O earth, earth, earth! Perhaps these words came like thunder to his soul. That they were spoken audibly we are assured from verse 7. His companions heard the voice.

Our Lord now arrests the persecuting zealot, calling him by name; the word never does us good until we find it spoken to us in particular. "Saul, Saul, why persecutest thou me?" Put the emphasis upon the word *why*, what evil have I done? Put it upon the word *persecutest*, why persecutest! I suppose Saul thought he was not persecuting. No, he was only putting the laws of the ecclesiastical court into execution. But Jesus, whose eyes are as a flame of fire, saw through the hypocrisy of his heart, that, notwithstanding his specious pretenses, all this proceeded from a persecuting spirit and secret enmity of heart against God; He therefore says, "Why persecutest thou *me?*" Put the emphasis upon the word *me*, Why persecutest thou me? Alas! Saul was not persecuting Christ, was he? He was only taking care to prevent innovations in the church and bringing a company of enthusiasts to justice, who otherwise would overturn the established constitution. But Jesus says, "Why persecutest thou me"! For what is done to Christ's disciples, He takes as done to Himself, whether it be good or whether it be evil. He that touches Christ's disciples touches the apple of His eye; they that persecute the followers of our Lord would persecute our Lord Himself, were He again to come and tabernacle among us.

I do not find that Saul gives any reason why he did persecute. No, he was struck dumb, as every persecutor will be when Jesus Christ puts the same question to them at the terrible day of judgment. But being pricked at the heart, no doubt with a sense not only of this, but of all his other offenses against the great God, he said, "Who art thou, Lord?" (v. 5). See how soon God can change the heart and voice of His most bitter enemies. Not many days ago, Saul was not only blaspheming Christ himself, but, as much as in him lay, compelling others to blaspheme also. But now, He who

before was an impostor is called Lord; "who art thou,
Lord?" This admirably points out the way in which
God's Spirit works upon the heart. It first powerfully
convinces of sin and of our damnable state and then
puts us upon inquiring after Jesus Christ. Saul being
struck to the ground, or pricked to the heart, cries out
after Jesus, "Who art thou, Lord?" Many of you that
were never so far made sensible of your damnable state
as to be made feelingly to seek after Jesus Christ were
never yet truly convicted by, much less converted to,
God. May the Lord who struck Saul effectually now
strike all my Christless hearers and set them upon
inquiring after Jesus as their all in all! Saul said, "Who
art thou, Lord? And the Lord said, I am Jesus, whom
thou persecutest" (v. 5). Never did any one inquire truly
after Jesus Christ but Christ made a saving discovery
of Himself to his soul. It should seem our Lord appeared to him in person, for Ananias afterward says,
"the Lord, even Jesus, that appeared unto thee in the
way as thou camest" (v. 17); though this may not only
imply Christ's meeting him in the way, it is not much
matter. It is plain Christ here speaks to him and says,
"I am Jesus whom thou persecutest."

It is remarkable how our Lord takes to Himself the
name of Jesus, for it is a name in which He delights. I
am Jesus, a Savior of My people, both from the guilt
and power of their sins; a "Jesus whom thou
persecutest." This seems to be spoken to convince Saul
more and more of his sin, and I doubt not that every
word was sharper than a two-edged sword and came
like so many daggers to his heart. O, how did these
words affect him! A Jesus! a Savior! and yet I am persecuting Him! This strikes him with horror, but then
the word *Jesus*, though he was a persecutor, might
give him some hope. However, our dear Lord, to convince Saul that he was to be saved by grace and that
He was not afraid of his power and enmity, tells him,
"It is hard for thee to kick against the pricks," as much
as to say, though he was persecuting, yet he could not
overthrow the church of Christ. Christ would sit as

King upon His holy hill of Zion; the malice of men or
devils should never be able to prevail against Him.

"And he trembling and astonished said, Lord, what
wilt thou have me to do?" (v. 6). Those who think Saul
had a discovery of Jesus made to his heart before think
that this question is the result of his faith and that he
now desires to know what he shall do out of gratitude
for what the Lord had done for his soul. In this sense it
may be understood, and I have made use of it as an
instance to prove that faith will work by love. But perhaps it may be more agreeable to the context if we
suppose that Saul had only some distant discovery of
Christ made to him and not a full assurance of faith.
We are told, "he trembling and astonished"—trembling
at the thoughts of his persecuting a Jesus and astonished at his own vileness and at the infinite condescen-
sion of this Jesus—cries out, "Lord, what wilt thou
have me to do?" Persons under soul-trouble and sore
conviction would be glad to do any thing or comply on
any terms to get peace with God. "Arise," says our
Lord, "and go into the city, and it shall be told thee
what thou shalt do."

And here we will leave Saul awhile and see what is
become of his companions. But what shall we say? God
is a sovereign agent; His sacred Spirit blows when and
where it listeth; He will have mercy on whom He will
have mercy (see Rom. 9:18). Saul is taken, but, as far
as we know to the contrary, his fellow travelers are left
to perish in their sins, for we are told that the men
who journeyed with him stood, indeed speechless, and
hearing a confused voice (Acts 9:7). I say a *confused*
voice, for so the word signifies and must be so inter-
preted in order to reconcile it with chapter 22, verse 9,
where Saul giving an account of these men, tells
Agrippa, "They heard not the voice of him that spake
to me." They heard a voice, a confused noise, but not
the articulate voice of Him that spoke to Saul and
therefore remained unconverted. For what are all ordi-
nances, all, even the most extraordinary dispensations
of providence, without Christ speaks to the soul in

them? Thus it is now under the word preached. Many, like Saul's companions, are sometimes so struck with the outgoings of God appearing in the sanctuary that they even stand speechless; they hear the preacher's voice but not the voice of the Son of God, who, perhaps, at the same time, is speaking effectually to many other hearts. This I have known often, and what shall we say to these things? O the depth of the sovereignty of God! It is past finding out. Lord, I desire to adore what I cannot comprehend. "Even so, Father: for so it seemed good in thy sight!" (Matt. 11:26).

But to return to Saul. The Lord bids him arise and go into the city, and we are told in verse 8 that "Saul arose from the earth; and when his eyes were opened [for he was so overpowered with the greatness of the light that shone upon them], he saw no man: but they led him by the hand, and brought him into Damascus," that very city which was to be the place of his executing or imprisoning the disciples of the Lord. "And he was three days without sight, and neither did eat nor drink" (Acts 9:9). But who can tell what horrors of conscience, what convulsion of soul, what deep and pungent convictions of sin he underwent during these three long days? It was this that took away his appetite (for who can eat or drink when under a sense of the wrath of God for sin?), and to be greatly employed hereafter, he must be greatly humbled now. Therefore the Lord leaves him three days groaning under the spirit of bondage and buffeted, no doubt, with the fiery darts of the Devil, that, being tempted like to his brethren, he might be able hereafter to succor those that were tempted. Had Saul applied to any of the blind guides of the Jewish church under these circumstances, they would have said he was mad or going beside himself, as many carnal teachers and blind Pharisees now deal with and so more and more distress poor souls laboring under awakening convictions of their damnable state. But God often at our first awakenings visits us with sore trials, especially those who are, like Saul, to shine in the church and to be used as instruments in bringing many sons to glory. Those who are to be highly exalted must first be deeply humbled, and this I speak for the comfort of those who may be now groaning under the spirit of bondage and perhaps, like Saul, can neither eat nor drink. I have generally observed that those who have had the deepest convictions have afterward been favored with the most precious communications and enjoyed most of the divine presence in their souls. This was afterward remarkably exemplified in Saul, who was three days without sight and neither did eat nor drink.

But will the Lord leave His poor servant in this distress? No. His Jesus (though Saul persecuted Him) promised and He will perform that it should be told him what he must do. "And there was a certain disciple at Damascus, named Ananias, and to him said the Lord in a vision, Ananias. And he said, Behold, I am here, Lord" (v. 10). What a holy familiarity is there between Jesus Christ and regenerate souls! Ananias had been used to such love visits and therefore knew the voice of his beloved. The Lord says, Ananias; Ananias says, "Behold, I am here, Lord." Thus it is that Christ now, as well as formerly, often talks with His children at sundry times and after divers manners, as a man talks with his friend. But what has the Lord to say to Ananias?

"And the Lord said unto him, Arise, and go into the street which is called Straight, and enquire in the house of Judas for one called Saul of Tarsus [see here for your comfort, O children of the most high God, what notice Jesus Christ takes of the street, and the house where His own dear servants lodge]: for, behold, he prayeth" (v. 11). But why is this ushered in with the word *behold?* What, was it such a wonder to hear that Saul was praying? Why, Saul was a Pharisee and therefore, no doubt, fasted and made long prayers. Since we are told that he profited above many of his equals, I doubt not that he was taken notice of for his gift in prayer. Yet it seems that before these three days Saul never prayed in his life. And why? Because before these three days he never felt himself a condemned creature.

He was alive in his own opinion because without a knowledge of the spiritual meaning of the law he felt not a want of, and therefore, before now, cried not after a Jesus. Consequently, though he might have said or made a prayer, as many Pharisees do in these days, he never uttered a prayer. But now, behold! he prayed indeed; this was urged as one reason why he was converted. None of God's children, as one observes, come into the world stillborn. Prayer is the very breath of a new creature. Therefore, if we are prayerless, we are Christless; if we never had the spirit of supplication, it is a sad sign that we never had the spirit of grace in our souls. You may be assured you never did pray unless you have felt yourselves sinners and seen the want of Jesus to be your Savior. May the Lord, whom I serve in the Gospel of His dear Son, prick you all to the heart, and may it be said of you all as it was of Saul—Behold, they pray!

The Lord goes on to encourage Ananias to go to Saul. He says, For he "hath seen in a vision a man named Ananias coming in, and putting his hand on him, that he might receive his sight" (v. 12). So that though Christ converted Saul immediately by Himself, yet He will carry on the work, thus begun, by a minister. Happy they who, under soul troubles, have such experienced guides and as well acquainted with Jesus Christ as Ananias was. You that have such, make much of and be thankful for them; you who have them not, trust in God, He will carry on His own work without them.

Doubtless, Ananias was a good man, but shall I commend him for his answer to our Lord? I commend him not, for he says, "Lord, I have heard by many of this man, how much evil he has done to thy saints at Jerusalem: and here he hath authority from the chief priests to bind all that call upon thy name" (vv. 13–14). I fear this answer proceeded from some relics of self-righteousness, as well as infidelity, that lay uncovered in the heart of Ananias. "Arise [said our Lord], and go into the street which is called Straight, and enquire in the house of Judas for one called Saul of Tarsus: for, behold, he prayeth" (v. 11)! One would think this was sufficient to satisfy him. But Ananias says, "Lord I have heard by many of this man [he seems to speak of him with much contempt, for even good men are apt to think too contemptuously of those who are yet in their sins] how much evil he hath done to thy saints in Jerusalem: and here he hath authority from the chief priests to bind all that call upon thy name." And what then, Ananias? Is anything too hard for the Lord? Who made thee to differ? Could not He who converted you convert him also? Surely Ananias here forgets himself or perhaps fears lest this man, who had authority from the chief priests to bind all that call upon Christ's name, should bind him also if he went to him. But the Lord silences all objections with a "Go thy way: for he is a chosen vessel unto me, to bear my name before the Gentiles, and kings, and the children of Israel: for I will shew him how great things he must suffer for my name's sake" (v. 15). Here God stops his mouth immediately by asserting His sovereignty and preaching to him the doctrine of election.

The frequent conversion of notorious sinners to God to me is one great proof, among a thousand others, of that precious but too much exploded and sadly misrepresented doctrine of God's electing love, for whence is it that such are taken, while thousands not near so vile die senseless and stupid? All the answer that can be given is, they are chosen vessels. "Go thy way [says God]: for he is a chosen vessel unto me, to bear my name before the Gentiles, and kings, and the children of Israel: for I will shew him how great things he must suffer for my name's sake." Observe what a close connection there is between doing and suffering for Christ. If any of my brethren in the ministry are present, let them hear what preferment we must expect if we are called out to work remarkably for God—not great prebendaries or bishoprics, but great sufferings for our Lord's name's sake; these are the fruits of our labor. He that will not contentedly suffer great things for preaching Christ is not worthy of Him. Suffering will

be found to be the best preferment when we are called
to give an account of our ministry at the great day.

I do not hear that Ananias quarreled with God concerning the doctrine of election. No; O that all good
men would, in this, learn of him! He "went his way,
and entered into the house; and putting his hands on
him said, Brother Saul." Just now it was "this man,"
now it is "Brother Saul" (v. 17). It is no matter what a
man has been if he be now a Christian; the same should
be our brother, our sister, and mother. God blots out
every convert's transgressions as with a thick cloud,
and so should we. The more vile a man has been, the
more should we love him when believing in Christ because Christ will be more glorified on his behalf. I
doubt not that Ananias was wonderfully delighted to
hear that so remarkable a persecutor was brought home
to God! I am persuaded he felt his soul immediately
united to him by love and therefore addresses him not
with, Thou persecutor, Thou murderer, that comest to
butcher me and my friends; but, "Brother Saul." It is
remarkable that the primitive Christians much used
the word *brother* and *brethren*. I know it is a term now
much in reproach, but those who despise it I believe
would be glad to be of our brotherhood when they see
us sitting at the right hand of the Majesty on high.
"Brother Saul, the Lord, even Jesus, that appeared unto
thee in the way as thou camest hath sent me, that
thou mightest receive thy sight, and be filled with the
Holy Ghost" (v. 17). At this time, we may suppose, he
laid his hands upon him. See the consequences.

"Immediately there fell from his eyes as it had been
scales: and he received sight forthwith" (v. 18), and not
only bodily, but spiritual sight. He emerged as it were
into a new world. He saw, and felt too, things unutter-
able. He felt a union of soul with God; he received the
spirit of adoption; he could now, with a full assurance
of faith, cry, "Abba, Father." Now was he filled with
the Holy Spirit and had the love of God shed abroad in
his heart; now were the days of his mourning ended;
now was Christ formed in his soul; now he could give

men and devils the challenge, knowing that Christ had justified him; now he saw the excellencies of Christ and esteemed Him the fairest among ten thousand. You only know how to sympathize with the apostle in his joy who, after a long night of bondage, have been set free by the Spirit and have received joy in the Holy Spirit. May all that are now mourning, as Saul was, be comforted in like manner!

The scales are now removed from the eyes of Saul's mind. Ananias has done that for him under God. He must now do another office—baptize him and so receive him into the visible church of Christ, a good proof to me of the necessity of baptism where it may be had. I find here, as well as elsewhere, that baptism is administered even to those who had received the Holy Spirit; Saul was convinced of this and therefore arose and was baptized. Now it is time for Ananias to recruit the outward man, which, by three days abstinence and spiritual conflicts, had been much impaired. We are therefore told, "when he had received meat, he was strengthened" (v. 19).

But O, with what comfort did the apostle now eat his food? I am sure it was with singleness, I am persuaded also with gladness, of heart. Why? He knew that he was reconciled to God; for my own part, did I not know how blind and flinty our hearts are by nature, I should wonder how anyone could eat even his common food with any satisfaction who has not some well grounded hope of his being reconciled to God. Our Lord intimates thus much to us, for in His glorious prayer, after He has taught us to pray for our daily bread, immediately He adds that petition, "forgive us our trespasses," as though our daily bread would do us no service unless we were sensible of having the forgiveness of our sins.

To proceed: Saul hath received meat and is strengthened, and whither will he go now? To see the brethren: "Then was Saul certain days with the disciples which were at Damascus" (v. 19). If we know and love Christ, we shall also love and desire to be acquainted with the brethren of Christ. We may generally know a man by his company. And though all are not saints that associate with saints (for tares will be always springing up among the wheat until the time of harvest), yet, if we never keep company, but are shy and ashamed of the despised children of God, it is a certain sign we have not yet experimentally learned Jesus or received Him into our hearts. My dear friends, be not deceived. If we are friends to the Bridegroom, we shall be friends to the children of the Bridegroom. Saul, as soon as he was filled with the Holy Spirit, was "certain days with the disciples which were at Damascus."

But who can tell what joy these disciples felt when Saul came among them! I suppose holy Ananias introduced him. I think I see the once persecuting zealot, when they came to salute him with a holy kiss, throwing himself upon each of their necks, weeping over them with floods of tears and saying, "O my brother, O my sister, can you forgive me? Can you give such a wretch as I the right hand of fellowship who intended to drag you behind me bound to Jerusalem?" Thus, I say, we may suppose Saul addressed himself to his fellow disciples. I doubt not that they were as ready to forgive and forget as Ananias was and saluted him with the endearing title of "Brother Saul." Lovely was this meeting. So lovely that it seemed Saul continued certain days with them to communicate experiences and to learn the way of God more perfectly, to pray for a blessing on his future ministry and to praise Christ Jesus for what He had done for their souls. Saul, perhaps, had sat certain years at the feet of Gamaliel, but undoubtedly learned more these certain days than he had learned before in all his life. It pleases me to think how this great scholar is transformed by the renewing of his mind—what a mighty change was here! That so great a man as Saul was—both as to his station in life and internal qualifications, and such a bitter enemy to the Christians—for him, I say, to go and be certain days with the people of this mad way and to sit quietly and be taught of illiterate men, as many of these disciples we may be sure were, what a substantial proof was this of the reality of his conversion!

What a hurry and confusion may we suppose the chief priests now were in! I warrant they were ready to cry out, What! is he also deceived? As for the common people who knew not the law and are accursed, for them to be carried away is no such wonder. But for a man bred up at the feet of Gamaliel, for such a scholar, such an enemy to the cause as Saul, for him to be led away with a company of silly, deceived men and women, surely it is impossible. We cannot believe it. But Saul soon convinces them of the reality of his becoming a fool for Christ's sake. For straightway, instead of going to deliver the letters from the high priest, as they expected, in order to bring the disciples that were at Damascus bound to Jerusalem, "he preached Christ in the synagogues, that he is the Son of God" (v. 20). This was another proof of his being converted. He not only conversed with Christians in private, but he preached Christ publicly in the synagogues. Especially, he insisted on the divinity of our Lord, proving, notwithstanding His state of humiliation, that He was really the Son of God.

But why did Saul preach Christ thus? Because he had felt the power of Christ upon his own soul. And here is the reason why Christ is so seldom preached and His divinity so slightly insisted on in our synagogues: because the generality of those that pretend to preach Him never felt a saving work of conversion upon their own souls. How can they preach unless they are first taught of and then sent by God! Saul did not preach Christ before he knew Him. No more should anyone else. An unconverted minister, though he could speak with the tongues of men and angels, will be but as sounding brass and tinkling cymbal to those whose senses are exercised to discern spiritual things. Ministers that are unconverted may talk and declaim of Christ and prove from books that He is the Son of God, but they cannot preach with the demonstration of the Spirit and with power unless they preach from experience and have had a proof of His divinity by a work of grace wrought upon their own souls. God forgive those who lay hands on an unconverted man, knowing that he is such. I would not do it for a thousand worlds. Lord Jesus, keep Your own faithful servants pure, and let them not be then partakers of other men's sins!

Such an instance as was Saul's conversion, we may be assured, must make a great deal of noise. Therefore, no wonder we are told in verse 21: "But all that heard him were amazed, and said; Is not this he that destroyed them who called on this name in Jerusalem, and came hither for that intent, that he might bring them bound to the chief priests?"

Thus it will be with all that appear publicly for Jesus Christ, and it is as impossible for a true Christian to be hid as a city built upon a hill. Brethren, if you are faithful, you must be reproached and have remarks made on you for Christ, especially if you have been remarkably wicked before your conversion. Your friends say, Is not this he or she who a little while ago would run to as great excess of riot and vanity as the worst of us all? What has turned your brain? Or if you have been close, false, formal hypocrites, as Saul was, they will wonder that you should be so deceived as to think you were not in a safe state before. No doubt, numbers were surprised to hear Saul, who was touching the law blameless, affirm that he was in a damnable condition (as in all probability he did) a few days before.

Brethren, you must expect to meet with many such difficulties as these. The scourge of the tongue is generally the first cross we are called to bear for the sake of Christ. Let not, therefore, this move you. It did not intimidate, no, it rather encouraged Saul.

Says the text, "But Saul increased the more in strength, and confounded the Jews which dwelt at Damascus, proving that this is very Christ" (v. 22). Opposition never yet did nor ever will hurt a sincere convert. There is nothing like opposition to make the man of God perfect. None but a hireling who cares not for the sheep will be affrighted at the approach or barking of wolves. Christ's ministers are as bold as lions. It is not for such men as they to flee.

And therefore (that I may draw toward a conclusion) let the ministers and disciples of Christ learn from Saul not to fear men or their revilings, but, like him, to increase in strength the more wicked men endeavor to weaken their hands. We cannot be Christians without being opposed. No; disciples in general must suffer; ministers in particular must suffer great things. But let not this move any of us from our steadfastness in the Gospel. He that stood by and strengthened Saul will also stand by and strengthen us. He is a God mighty to save all that put their trust in Him. If we look up with an eye of faith, we, as well as the first martyr Saint Stephen, may see Jesus standing at the right hand of God ready to assist and protect us. Though the Lord's seat is in heaven, yet He has respect to His saints in an especial manner when they are suffering here on earth. Then the Spirit of Christ and of glory rests upon their souls. And, if I may speak my own experience, I never enjoy more rich communications from God than when despised and rejected of men for the sake of Jesus Christ. However little they may design it, my enemies are my greatest friends. What I most fear is a calm, but the enmity which is in the hearts of natural men against Christ will not suffer them to be quiet long. No; as I hope the work of God will increase, so the rage of men and devils will increase also. Let us put on, therefore, the whole armor of God. Let us not fear the face of men. Let us fear Him only who can destroy both body and soul in hell. I say to you, let us fear Him alone. You see how soon God can stop the fury of His enemies.

You have just now heard of a proud, powerful zealot stopped in his full career, struck down to the earth with a light from heaven, converted by the almighty power of efficacious grace, and thereupon zealously promoting—no, resolutely suffering for—the faith that once with threatenings and slaughters he endeavored to

destroy. Let this teach us to pity and pray for our
Lord's most inveterate enemies. Who knows but in answer thereunto our Lord may give them repentance to
life! Most think that Christ had respect to Stephen's
prayer when He converted Saul. Perhaps for this reason God suffers His adversaries to go on that His good-
ness and power may shine more bright in their
conversions.

But let not the persecutors of Christ take encouragement from this to continue in their opposition. Remember, though Saul was converted, yet the high priest
and Saul's companions were left dead in trespasses
and sins. If this should be your case, you will of all
men be most miserable. For persecutors have the low-
est place in hell. And if Saul was struck to the earth by
a light from heaven, how will you be able to stand
before Jesus Christ when He comes in terrible majesty
to take vengeance on all those who have persecuted
His Gospel? Then the question, "Why persecuted thou
me?" will cut you through and through. The secret enmity of your hearts shall be then detected before men
and angels, and you shall be doomed to dwell in the
blackness of darkness forevermore. Kiss the Son therefore, lest He be angry. For even you may yet find mercy
if you believe on the Son of God. Though you persecute
Him, yet He will be your Jesus.

I cannot despair of any of you when I find a Saul
among the disciples at Damascus. What though your
sins are as scarlet, the blood of Christ shall wash them
as white as snow. Having much to be forgiven, despair
not; only believe, and like Saul, of whom I have now
been speaking, love much. He counted himself the
chiefest sinner of all and therefore labored more
abundantly than all. Who is there among you fearing
the Lord? Whose hearts has the Lord now opened to
hearken to the voice of His poor unworthy servant?
Surely the Lord will not let me preach in vain. Who is
the happy soul that is this day to be washed in the
blood of the Lamb? Will no poor sinner take
encouragement from Saul to come to Jesus Christ? You

are all thronging round, but which of you will touch the Lord Jesus? What a comfort will it be to Saul, and to your own souls, when you meet him in heaven to tell him that hearing of his was a means, under God, of your conversion! Doubtless it was written for the encouragement of all poor returning sinners; he himself tells us so. For "I obtained mercy, that in me first Jesus Christ might shew forth all longsuffering, for a pattern to them which should hereafter believe" (1 Tim. 1:16). Were Saul here himself, he would tell you so, indeed he would. But being dead, by this account of his conversion, he yet speaks. O that God may speak by it to your hearts! O that the arrows of God might this day stick fast in your souls and you be made to cry out, "Who art thou, Lord?" Are there any such among you? I think I feel something of what this Saul felt when he said, "I travail in birth again until Christ be formed in you" (Gal. 4:19). O come, come away to Jesus on whom Saul believed, and then I care not if the high priests issue out never so many writs or injuriously drag me to a prison. The thoughts of being instrumental in saving you will make me sing praises even at midnight. And I know you will be my joy and crown of rejoicing when I am delivered from this earthly prison and meet you in the kingdom of God hereafter.

Saul Self-Contrasted

Joseph Parker (1830–1902) was one of England's most popular preachers. Largely self-educated, Parker had pulpit gifts that soon moved him into leadership among the Congregationalists. He was a fearless and imaginative preacher who attracted both common people and the aristocracy, and he was particularly a "man's preacher." His *People's Bible* is a collection of the shorthand reports of the sermons and prayers Parker delivered as he preached through the entire Bible in seven years (1884–1891). He pastored the Poultry Church, London, later called the City Temple, from 1869 until his death.

This sermon is taken from *The Ark of God*, published in 1877 by S. W. Partridge and Co., London.

Joseph Parker

3

SAUL SELF-CONTRASTED

Acts 9:1–22

WHAT WONDERFUL CONTRASTS THERE are in this narrative in reference to the character of Saul of Tarsus! He is not the same man throughout, and yet he is the same. The contrasts are so sharp, and, indeed, so violent, as almost to make him into another man altogether.

From Persecution to Prayer

For example, take the first of these contrasts, and you will find that Saul, who went out to persecute remained to pray. The first verse reads, "And Saul, yet breathing out threatenings and slaughter"! and in the eleventh verse occurs the remarkable expression, "Behold, he prayeth"! He breathed hotly. The breath of his nostrils was a fierce blast that burned the air. How changed in a little time! for his face is turned upward to heaven, and its very look is a pleading supplication. What has occurred? These effects must be accounted for. Have they any counterpart in our own observation and experience? Have any of us passed from fierceness to gentleness, from drunkenness to sobriety, from darkness to light, from blasphemy to worship? Then we understand what is meant by this most startling contrast. There may be others who have advanced so quietly and gradually as to find no such contrast in their own consciousness and experience, but we must not judge the experience of the whole by the experience of the part. This is precisely the work that Christianity undertakes to do. It undertakes to cool your breath, to take the fire out of your blood, to subdue your rancor and your malignity, and to clasp your hands in childlike plea and prayer at your Father's feet. Such is the continual miracle of Christianity. The religion of Jesus Christ would have nothing to do if this were not to be accomplished. Jesus makes the lion lie down with the lamb, and He causes the child to hold the fierce beast and to put its hand with impunity on the cockatrice's den. Other miracles He has ceased to perform, but this continual and infinite surprise is the standing miracle and the standing testimony of Christ.

From Threatening to Proving

Take the second contrast, which is quite as remarkable. When Saul was a Pharisee he persecuted; when Saul became a Christian we read in the twenty-second verse that he proved. How many miles of the moral kind lie between the word *persecuted* and the word *proved?* Yet this is distinctly in the line of Christian purpose and heavenly intent. As a Pharisee he said, "Destroy Christianity by destroying Christians. Bind them; put an end to this pestilence. Do not stand it any longer. Open your prison doors, and I will fill your dungeons, and we will bring this new and mischievous heresy to a speedy termination." Such was his first policy. Having seen Jesus and felt His touch and entered into His Spirit, what does he say? Does he now say, "The persecution must be turned in the other direction; I have been persecuting the wrong parties; now I find it is you Jews, Pharisees, Sadducees, that must be manacled and fettered and put an end to. I change my policy, and I persecute you, every man and woman of you"? Nothing of the kind. Observe this miracle, admire it, and let it stand before you as an argument invincible and complete. What is Saul's tone now? Standing with the scrolls open before him, he reasons and mightily contends; he becomes a vehement and luminous speaker of Christian truth. He increases the more in strength, proving that this is the Christ. Has all the persecuting temper gone? Yes, every whit of it. Why did he not prove to the Christians, in his unconverted state, that they were mistaken? When he was not a converted man, he never thought of proving anything. He had a rough, short, and easy method with heretics—stab them, burn them, drown them, bind them in darkness, and let them die of hunger! Now that he is a converted man, he becomes a reasoner. He stands up with an argument as his only weapon, persuasion as his only iron, entreaty and supplication as the only chains with which he would bind his opponents.

What has happened? Something vital must have occurred. Is there not a counterpart of all this in our own individual experience and in civilized history? Do not men always begin vulgarly and end with refinement? Is not the first rough argument a thrust with cold iron or a blow with clenched fist? Does not history teach us that such methods are utterly unavailing in the extinction or the final arrest of erroneous teaching? Christianity is a moral plea. Christianity burns no man. Wherein professing Christians have resorted to the block and the stake and to evil instruments, they have proved disloyal to their Master, and they have forgotten the spirit of His Cross. Christianity is a plea, a persuasion, an appeal, an address to reason, conscience, heart, and to everything that makes a man a man. Christianity uses no force and asks for no force to be used on its behalf. You cannot make men pray by force of arms. You cannot drive your children to church, except in the narrowest and shallowest sense of the term. You may convince men of their error and lead men to the sanctuary and, through the confidence of their reason and their higher sentiments, you may conduct them to your own noblest conclusions. How far is it from persecuting to praying? From threatening and slaughter to proving? That distance Christ took Saul, who only meant to go from Jerusalem to Damascus, some hundred and thirty-six miles. Christ took him a longer journey; He swept him around the whole circle of possibility. He made him accomplish the entire journey that lies between persecution and prayer, slaughter and argument. It is thus that Jesus Christ makes us do more than we intended to do. He meets us on the way of our own choice and graciously takes us on a way of His own.

From Destroyer to Blind Man

Look at the third contrast, which is as notable as the other two. In the opening of the narrative Saul was a strong man, the strongest of the band, the chief without whose presence the band would dissolve. His nostrils are dilated with anger. His eye burns with a fire that expresses the supreme purpose of his heart. Nothing stands between him and the accomplishment of his purpose. The caravan road from Jerusalem to Damascus, supposing that he took that road, required some six days to traverse it. Saul knew not the lapse of time, so high-strung was his energy and so resolute his purpose. And in this same narrative, not further on than the eighth verse, we read of the great persecutor, that "they led him by the hand." What has happened? We thought he would have gone into the city like a storm; he went in like a blind beggar! We thought he would have been met at the city gate as the great destroyer of heresy; he was led by the hand like a helpless cripple! Woe to the strength that is not heaven-born! Such so-called power will wither away. When we are weak then are we strong. Saul will one day teach us that very doctrine. Really understood, Saul was a stronger man when he was being led by the hand than when he breathed out threatenings and slaughter against the disciples of the Lord. You are mightier when you pray than when you persecute. You are stronger when you prove your argument than when you seek to smite your opponent. Something will come of this. Such violences have high moral issues.

Glimpses of Jesus

Turning to another aspect of the case, we see two or three most beautiful and pathetic glimpses of Jesus Christ Himself. He ascended, yet He said, "I am with you alway, even unto the end of the age" (my translation). There we find Him leaving, yet not leaving; not visible, yet watchful; looking upon Saul every day and looking at the same time upon His redeemed church night and day, the whole year round. Events are not happening without His knowledge; the story of all the ages is written in heaven. He knows your persecuting purpose; He understands well enough what you are doing to interrupt the cause of truth and the progress of Christian knowledge. Jesus Christ knows all your antagonistic plans, thoughts, purposes, and devices. His eye is upon you. As for you Christians, He knows your sufferings, your oppositions, your daily contentions, your painful striving; He knows exactly through how much tribulation you are moving onward to the kingdom.

Not only is He living and watchful, but in the case of Saul himself Jesus Christ was compassionate. Listen to the words that He addressed to Saul: "It is hard for thee to kick against the pricks" (Acts 9:5). He pitied the poor ox that struck its limbs against the sharp and piercing goads. There is nothing destructive in this criticism. There is the spirit of Christ in this remark. Yes, this expostulation repeats the prayer of His dying breath, and shows Him to be "the same yesterday, today, and forever" (Heb. 13:8). He does not bind Saul with his own chain; He throws upon him the happy spell of victorious love.

Not only is He living, watchful, and compassionate, He is consistent. He said to Ananias, "I will shew him how great things he must suffer for my name's sake." When Jesus called His disciples to Him and ordained them to go out into the world, He laid before them a black picture; He kept back nothing of the darkness. He told His disciples that they would be persecuted, dragged up before the authorities, and cruelly treated; now, when He comes to add another to the number, He repeats the ordination charge that He addressed to the first band.

Has the Vision Ceased?

All these things were seen in a vision. Say some of you, "We have no visions now." Have we not? How can we? We may eat and drink all visions away. The glutton and the drunkard can have nothing but nightmare.

A materialistic age can only have a materialistic religion. If men will satisfy every appetite, indulge every desire to satiety, turn the day into night and the night into a long revel, they cannot wonder if the vision should have departed from their lives. We may grieve the Spirit, we may quench the Spirit; we may so eat and drink and live as to divest the mind of its wings and becloud the whole horizon of the fancy. But is it true that the vision has ceased? It may be so within a narrow sense, but not in its true spiritual intent and thought. Even now we speak about strong impressions, impulses we cannot account for, movements, desires of the mind that lie beyond our control. Even now we are startled by unexpected combinations of events. Even now we have a mysterious side to life as well as an obvious and patent side. What if the religious mind should see in such realities the continued Presence and the continued vision that gladdened the early church? If you would see the spiritual, you must keep down the material. If you would have visions, you must banish the basely substantial. If you would have high dreamings and noble revelations, you must mortify the flesh.

See from this conversion how true it is that Christianity does not merely alter a man's intellectual views or modify a man's moral prejudices. Christianity never makes a little alteration in a man's thinking and action. Christianity makes new hearts, new creatures, and not new plans and new habits only. Other reformers may change a habit now and again, may modify a prejudice, attempt a purpose with some benign and gracious intent; but this Redeemer, who gave Himself, the just for the unjust, who bought with the blood of His own heart, does not make a little difference in our intellectual attitudes and our moral purposes. He wants us to be born again. "If any man be in Christ, he is a new creature: old things are passed away; behold, all things are become new" (2 Cor. 5:17). There drop from his eyes as it were scales, and, with a pure heart, he sees a pure God.

NOTES

Paul's Visit to Jerusalem to See Peter

Alexander Whyte (1836–1921) was known as "the last of the Puritans," and certainly his sermons were surgical as he magnified the glory of God and exposed the sinfulness of sin. He succeeded the noted Robert S. Candlish as pastor of Free Saint George's and reigned from that influential Edinburgh pulpit for nearly forty years. He loved to "dig again in the old wells" and share with his people truths learned from the devotional masters of the past. His evening Bible courses attracted the young people and led many into a deeper walk with God.

This sermon is taken from *Bible Characters from the Old and New Testaments*, reprinted in 1990 by Kregel Publications.

Alexander Whyte

4

PAUL'S VISIT TO JERUSALEM TO SEE PETER

PUT YOURSELF BACK INTO Paul's place. Suppose yourself born in Tarsus, brought up at Gamaliel's feet in Jerusalem, and keeping the clothes of Stephen's executioners. Think of yourself as a blasphemer and a persecutor and injurious. And—then imagine yourself apprehended of Christ Jesus, driven of the Spirit into the wilderness of Arabia, and coming back with all your bones burning within you to preach Jesus Christ and Him crucified. But, all the time, you have never once seen your Master in the flesh as His twelve disciples had seen Him. He had been for thirty years with His mother and His sisters and His brethren in Galilee. And then He had been for three years with the Twelve and the seventy. But Paul had been born out of due time. And thus it was that Paul went up to Jerusalem to see Peter. Paul had a great desire to see Peter about all that before he began his ministry. And you would have had that same great desire, and so would I.

At the same time, even with the prospect of seeing Peter, it must have taken no little courage on Paul's part to face Judea and Jerusalem again—to face the widows and the orphans of the men he had put to death in the days of his ignorance and unbelief. To Paul the very streets of Jerusalem were still wet with that innocent blood. Led in by Peter, Paul sat at the same Lord's Table and ate the same bread and drank the same wine with both old and young communicants who had not yet put off their garments of mourning because of Paul. Deliver me from blood-guiltiness, O God of my salvation. Then will I teach transgressors

Your ways. Do good in Your good pleasure to Zion; build the walls of Jerusalem. And thus it was that, to the end of his days, Paul was always making elections for those same poor saints that were in Jerusalem. Paul would have pensioned every one of them out of his own pocket had he been able. But how could he do that off a needle and a pair of shears? And thus it was that he begged so incessantly for the fatherless families that he had made fatherless in Judea and in Jerusalem. Now, if any of you have ever made any woman a widow or any child an orphan or done anything of that remorseful kind, do not flee the country. You cannot do it, and you need not try. Remain where you are. Go back to the place. Go back often in imagination, if not in your bodily presence. Do the very utmost that in you lies to repair the irreparable wrong that you did long ago. And, when you cannot redeem that dreadful damage, commit it to Him who can redeem both it and you. And say to Him continually: Count me a partner with You. And put that also down to my account.

"To see Peter," our Authorized Version is made to say. "To visit" Peter, the Revised Version is made to say. And, still, to help out all that acknowledged lameness, the Revised margin is made to say, "to become acquainted with" Peter. But Paul would not have gone so far, at that time at any rate, to see Peter or anyone else—anyone else but Peter's Master. But to see Him even once, as He was in the flesh, Paul would have gone from Damascus to Jerusalem on his hands and his knees. "I went up to Jerusalem to *history* Peter," is what Paul really says. Only, that is not good English. But far better bad English than an utterly meaningless translation of such a text. "To interview Peter," is not good English either, but it conveys Paul's meaning exactly. The great Greek historians employ Paul's very identical word when they tell their readers the pains they took to get firsthand information before they began to write their books. "I went up to interrogate and to cross-question Peter all about our Lord," that would be rough English indeed, but it would be far better

than so feebly to say, "to see Peter," which positively
hides from his readers what was Paul's real errand to
Jerusalem and to Peter.

Had Landor been led to turn his fine dramatic genius and his ripe scholarship to Scriptural subjects, he
would, to a certainty, have given us the conversations
that took place for fifteen days between Peter and Paul.
Landor's Epictetus and Seneca, his Diogenes and Plato,
his Melanchthon and Calvin, his Galileo and Milton
and a Dominican, and his Dante and Beatrice, are all
among his masterpieces. But his Paul and Peter, and
his Paul and James the brother of our Lord, and especially his Paul and the mother of our Lord, would have
eclipsed clean out of sight his most classical composi-
tions. For on no possible subject was Peter so ready
always to speak, to all comers, as just about his Master. And never before nor since had Peter such a hun-
gry hearer as just his present visitor and interrogator
from Arabia and Damascus. Peter began by telling Paul
all about that day when his brother Andrew so burst
in upon him about the Messiah. And then that day
only second to it, on the Lake of Gennesaret. And then
Matthew the publican's feast, and so on, until Peter
soon saw what it was that Paul had come so far to
hear. And then he went on with the good Samaritan
and the lost piece of silver and the lost sheep and the
lost son. For fifteen days and fifteen nights this went
on until the two prostrate men took their shoes off
their feet when they entered the Garden of Gethsemane.
And both at the cock-crowing and at Calvary, Peter
and Paul wept so sore that Mary herself and Mary
Magdalene did not weep like it.

Now, just trust me and tell me what you would have
asked Peter about his Master. Would you have asked
anything? How far would you go tonight to have an
interview with Peter? Honestly, have you any curiosity
at all about Jesus Christ, either as He is in heaven
now or as He was on earth then? Really and truly, do
you ever think about Him and imagine Him and what
He is saying and doing? Or are you like John Bunyan,

who never thought whether there was a Christ or no? If you would tell me two or three of the questions you would have put to Peter, I would tell you in return just who and what you are, just how you stand tonight to Jesus Christ and how He stands to you, what He thinks and says about you and intends toward you.

And then if Mary, the mother of our Lord, was still in this world, it is certain to me that Paul both saw her in James's house and kissed her hand and called her blessed. You may depend upon it that Mary did not remain very long away from James's house after his conversion. It was all very good to have a lodging with the disciple whom Jesus loved, until her own slow-hearted son believed. But I put it to you who are mothers in Israel to put yourselves in Mary's place in those days and to say if you would have been to be found anywhere, by that time, but in the house of your own believing son. And what more sure and certain than that God, here again, revealed His Son to Paul out of Mary's long-hidden heart. I have the most perfect and at firsthand assurance of all these things from them that "were eyewitnesses, and ministers of the word," says Paul's physician and private secretary. Nowhere, at any rate, in the whole world could that miraculous and mystery-laden woman have found such another heart as Paul's into which to pour out all that had been for so long sealed up in her hidden heart. "Whether we were in the body, or out of the body, as she told me about Nazareth, and as I told her about Damascus and Arabia, I cannot tell: God knoweth."

"From the Old Testament point of view," says Bengel in his own striking and suggestive way, "the progress is made from the knowledge of Christ to the knowledge of Jesus. From the New Testament point of view, the progress is made from the knowledge of Jesus to the knowledge of Christ." And have we not ourselves already seen how Paul's progress was made? Paul's progress was made from the knowledge of Jesus of Nazareth risen from the dead to the knowledge of the Son of God, and then from the knowledge of both back to the knowledge of the holy child Jesus and the holy man Jesus, as He was known to His mother, to James His brother, and to Peter His so intimate disciple. Paul went "back to Jesus," as the saying sometimes is; but when he went back he took back with him all the knowledge of the Son of God that he has put into his epistles, aye, and much more than the readers of his epistles were able to receive. And God's way with Paul is His best way with us also. You will never read the four Gospels with true intellectual understanding and with true spiritual appreciation until you have first read and understood and appreciated Paul's epistles. But after you have had God's Son revealed in you by means of Paul's epistles, you will then be prepared for all that Matthew and Mark and Luke and John have to tell you about the Word made flesh in their day. Paul's hand holds the true key to all the mysteries that are hid in the Prophets and in the Psalms and in the Gospels. Take back Paul with you, and all the prophecies and all the types of the Old Testament and all the wonderful works of God in the New Testament—His Son's sinless conception, His miracles, His teaching and preaching, His agony in the garden, His death on the cross, and His resurrection and ascension—will all fall into their natural and necessary places. It is in the very same order in which the great things of God were revealed to Paul and apprehended by Paul that they will best be revealed to us and best apprehended by us. First our conversion and then the Pauline, Patristic, and Puritan doctrine of the Son of God, and then all that is taken back by us to the earthly life of our Blessed Lord as it is told to us by the four Evangelists. Damascus, Arabia, Jerusalem—this, in our day also, is the God-guided progress in which the true successors of the apostle Paul are still traveling in their spiritual experience and in their evangelical scholarship.

A Drama in Four Acts

James S. Stewart (1896–1990) pastored three churches in Scotland before becoming professor of theology at the University of Edinburgh (1936) and then professor of New Testament (1946). But he was a professor who preached, a scholar who applied biblical truth to the needs of common people, and a theologian who made doctrine practical and exciting. He published several books of lectures and biblical studies including *A Man in Christ* and *Heralds of God*. His two finest books of sermons are *The Gates of New Life* and *The Strong Name*.

This sermon is taken from *The Gates of New Life*, published in Edinburgh in 1937 by T. & T. Clark.

James S. Stewart

5

A DRAMA IN FOUR ACTS

Take Mark, and bring him with thee: for he is profitable
to me for the ministry (2 Timothy 4:11).

THE STORY OF JOHN Mark, the deserter who made good,
could be written as a drama in four acts. But first, by
way of prologue to the drama, a question arises. How
came Mark to be accompanying Paul and Barnabas on
their hazardous adventures? This is easily enough
explained. There are three facts to remember.

The first is that Barnabas was his own cousin and
was no doubt eager to give the younger man a share in
the great work of carrying Christ's commission across
the world.

The second is that John Mark came from a home that
had played an outstanding part in the life of the church
from the first. His mother, Mary, had put her house at
the disposal of the Jerusalem Christians. It was there,
in an upper room of her house, that they met for weekly
worship. It was thither that Peter had made his way on
his dramatic escape from prison. Indeed, the probability
is that it was this same upper room that had seen the
Last Supper on the night of Calvary and the coming of
the Spirit at Pentecost and the birth of the Christian
church. Mark was the son of that home. Happy the
young man who begins life in a home where God has an
altar and Jesus is a familiar friend!

But we can go farther. The third fact is that it is at
least possible that Mark himself had been a secret disciple of Jesus. You will remember how his gospel, when
it comes to describe Gethsemane, mentions a mysterious young man who was in the garden on the night
when Jesus was arrested, who was almost arrested
himself, and escaped only by fleeing and leaving his

cloak behind him in the soldiers' hands. None of the other Evangelists mentions the incident, and tradition says that the young man was Mark himself, who put this personal touch into his gospel like an artist painting in his signature very faintly in an inconspicuous corner of his picture. However that may be, it is certain that he had been in close touch with the Christian leaders from the first. Hence we are not surprised to find him setting out with Paul and Barnabas on the first great Gospel campaign.

Act 1: Recantation

So we pass on from the prologue to Act 1 of the drama. This act bears the title *Recantation*. To begin with, all went well. Mark felt he had found his vocation. There was all the glamour of novelty about new places to visit, new friendships to make, new claims to stake out for Christ. But as the days went on, one thought began to trouble him. Were they not wandering too far from their base? Paul, with his far horizons and beckoning visions, seemed determined to carry the campaign into the unfamiliar and dangerous hinterland of Asia. Mark had not bargained for this. "The risk is far too great," he told himself, "it is not worth it! I must remonstrate with Paul." But when he endeavored to raise his objections, he found that he could scarce say a word, for there was something in Paul's face—a burning, passionate eagerness and a glowing resolute determination—that silenced his stammered protests. There seemed no alternative; he must go on. But all the time his nerve was beginning to fail him, and he knew it. What a wild, savage, God-forsaken land this was, and up among those mountain fastnesses what nameless perils might be lurking! And Jerusalem was so far away and his heart so terribly homesick! Many a night he would have given anything just to have heard the temple bells again or to have stood on Olivet and seen the sun flaming down the western sky. So the struggle went on in Mark's soul, until at last there came a crisis.

It was in the dead of night, and Paul and Barnabas were asleep; Mark was wakeful and was striding up and down alone, by himself in the dark. Take a long look at him, I beg you—for there is a man at the crossroads with Christ, a soul facing one of those decisive hours that come to all of us sooner or later. "I can't go on," he is saying. "I ought never to have come. O home, home—I'm weary for my home!"

And then another voice speaks, very quietly and tenderly, and it is the voice of Jesus.

"You are not going to leave Me, My friend? You surely can't be leaving Me now? Do you not love Me any more?"

And the man blurts out, "Yes, Lord, I do, you know I do! With all my heart I love you. How can you say such a thing? But, Lord, I don't think I was built for this. I'm not a Paul or a Barnabas, I'm not like them with their iron nerves and their lion hearts—I'm just one of your ordinary people, Jesus, and it is asking too much of me!"

Then again the quiet voice speaks, but sadly now— "I do not compel you, friend. You are free to return if you must. But I died for you, My son, and this is hard, hard for Me!"

"But don't you see, Lord, I can't go on? You must see that. I have tried my best, I have indeed, but I am not made for this kind of life, and it is not fair to ask me. Can't you understand?"

And at that a new voice, a third voice, comes breaking in—the voice of the Tempter.

"Let Christ go, then. Let Him go! Sell Him and be done with it. Recant, man, recant!"

And then a great silence. But in the morning, when Paul and Barnabas rose to continue their journey, there was no John Mark there. And they went on their way alone. The tragedy of a soul's recantation!

Now I know what some of us are thinking. All this was long, long ago. Conditions have changed completely. Christian discipleship is a far simpler affair today. No danger of our deserting Christ through fear!

But are we sure? Suppose we single out one particular

brand of fear. What about the fear of unpopularity, of being left on the shelf (as we say), of being passed over or made to suffer for our convictions? Does that never breed deserters?

Let me for one moment speak directly to the young men and women here tonight. Have you never stood at this particular crossroads with Christ, finding yourself suddenly confronted with the choice either to stand up for Jesus and let the world's good graces go, or else to muffle your Christianity and square the world and keep the favor of some social set? Perhaps you had only five minutes or less to make up your mind, to decide whether the flag was to be run to the top of the mast and held there resolutely in defiance of the consequences or discreetly hauled down and pushed away out of sight. "Men of Athens," exclaimed Socrates, "I hold you in the highest reverence and love; but I am going to obey God rather than you!" It takes some courage to do that in this modern age as much as in ancient Athens. It takes some grit and loyalty to do it—in social circle or shop or factory or club. When Wilberforce rose to speak in the House of Commons, "Ah," said a sneering member, "the honorable and religious gentleman!" That sort of thing stings, and there is a bit of us—"the natural man," Paul called it—which hates being stung and would rather do anything, would even blunder into open disloyalty and sin against God's Christ than stand out against the conventions of the world or the opinion of our fellowmen.

Unpopularity—that is one fear at least which still has the power to make souls desert from Christ. And there are others, the fear of sacrifice, for example, the fear of losing ambitions on which our hearts are set, the fear of having to give up something in thought, desire, or habit that we know ought to be given up (this is one of the sternest struggles of life, and until a man has fought through it he is not right with Christ), the fear of God's daily discipline, the fear of the cross. Is there one of us here who will dare point a condemning finger at John Mark or cast the first stone? Are we not all in this together? Yes, in some degree we have all played our part in this first tragic act—the act of recantation.

Act 2: Remorse

We go on now to Act 2, and this bears the title *Remorse*. Here we see Mark back in Jerusalem. The homesick man has come home. Away yonder among the mountains of Asia he had thought, "If only I could see Jerusalem, how happy I should be!" Well, here he is in Jerusalem. Is he happy now? Look at him.

People sometimes say a house is haunted. Perhaps, years before, some dark deed was perpetrated there, and the place has never thrown off its evil, sinister reputation. No prospective tenants come knocking at its door. It stands deserted and uncared for, and weeds and nettles block the garden paths. Passersby cast furtive glances at it in the daytime, and in the night the wind moans eerily around its walls, like the moaning of the ghosts of the dead. So sometimes the house of life, the soul, is haunted; ghosts of memory walk there, clanking their chains in the dark, shadows of old, unhappy, far-off things and wild regrets.

> In the night, in the night
> When thou liest alone,
> Ah! the ghosts that make moan
> From the days that are sped:
> The old dreams, the old deeds,
> The old wound that still bleeds,
> And the face of the dead,
> In the night.

That was John Mark back in Jerusalem. Everything was the same—the streets, his home, the temple bells, the sun flaming down behind Olivet, everything the same—yet somehow there was a subtle difference. All the dear familiar things had lost their savor. Happy in Jerusalem? Call him rather the most wretched man on earth. After recantation, remorse. Does it not always happen? Thomas Cranmer, Archbishop of Canterbury in the sixteenth century, recanted his faith in prison. "Sign that!" they said to him, thrusting a written document into his hands. But when he began to read it, "No," he burst out, "'tis a downright denial of my Christ! I will not sign." "Sign it or die," they threatened, and kept badgering him and torturing him, until in a weak moment he yielded and took the pen and wrote his name. But when it was done, the horror of his betrayal leaped upon his soul, and he looked at the right hand that had signed the name. Had not Jesus said, "If thy right hand offend thee, cut it off" (Matt. 5:30)? And for days and nights he was tormented with remorse. He would gladly have taken a knife and severed that traitor hand. And when at last, in spite of his recantation, they led him out to die and the vast throng swarmed around the martyr pyre to see the end, he stood and thrust his right arm first into the flames. "This unworthy hand," he said, "this which hath sinned, having signed the writing, must be the first to suffer"; and he held it there until it was blackened and consumed, then plunged into the fire himself.

Words cannot measure the remorse that gripped John Mark in Jerusalem, but the grip of it was agony. "Would God I might live those days through again!" he thought. "If only the thing had never happened! O God of mercy, turn time back, I beg, set me where I was before this dreadful thing occurred. I can't have been myself then! For I do love Jesus. I swear I love Him still. Lord, give me that bad hour back!"

One of Squire's fine poems depicts a man who has persistently neglected a dear one. Always he has been meaning to write, to send the long-looked-for letter, and always in the press of business he has kept putting it off. "Tomorrow I will do it," he tells himself, "certainly I will write tomorrow," but it is never done. And then one day a message comes. He tears it open; she is dead. And as he stands there staring at the words, remorse rushes in like a flood. "It shall not be today," he cries. "It shall not! It is still yesterday. I'll wrest the sun back in its course! It is still yesterday.

There is time still—there must be time!" Poor, unhappy soul! For

> The sun moves. Our onward course is set.
> There will be time for nothing but regret,
> And the memory of things done!

"You don't know," cries the chaplain in Shaw's *Saint Joan*, breaking in wildly after he had consented to the saint's death and had stood and watched her die, "you haven't seen: it is so easy to talk when you don't know. But when it is brought home to you; when you see the thing you have done; when it is blinding your eyes, stifling your nostrils, tearing your heart, then—then— O God, take away this sight from me! O Christ, deliver me from this fire that is consuming me! She cried to Thee in the midst of it: Jesus! Jesus! Jesus! She is in Thy bosom; and I am in hell for evermore."

After recantation—remorse!

So with John Mark. I think I can see him at night unable to sleep, rising from his bed, pacing to and fro in that upper room of many memories. "Where are Paul and Barnabas tonight?" he is wondering. "And where is Jesus?" I see him going down a Jerusalem street at noonday, and now and again people—Christian brethren of his own—look strangely at him as he passes, then turn and point: "See, there is the man who deserted! Would you believe it?" I see him at last one day sitting at the Communion Table. He is listening dully to the familiar words, "This is My body, broken for you. This is My blood, shed for you"; then the bread comes around and then the cup. But just as he lifts it, something happens. He pauses and looks at that cup in his hand, for within him a voice has begun to speak—a voice unheard by any of the others there, heard only in Mark's own soul. "This is Christ's blood," says the voice. "And if this is blood in the cup, and if it is the blood of Jesus, and if it was given for you, then what—in the name of all that is honorable—are you doing here? Jesus is out on the lonely, dangerous ways, seeking the lost and the perishing, and this is the blood of that agony. Will you dare to drink it—you? Look well into that cup, Mark, for you are crucifying Christ afresh, and there are drops of the blood of that second crucifixion in it. Look well into the cup!" And the man sits with the cup in his hand, staring at it (have we ever sat like that, confronted with the agony of Jesus and knowing that some unclean thought of ours, some selfish slackness, some wretched little self-indulgence, was the cause of it?). Then I see him suddenly setting the cup down untasted, rising from the table, and leaving the room—and that very night, do you know where he is? Out from Jerusalem, out on the great north road, with his face set toward Paul and Barnabas and Christ again!

There is an old Gaelic proverb that says, "If you cannot get back to the place where you were born, try to get within seeing distance of it." I would add to that: If you cannot get back to the place where you were first born into the life in God, get within seeing distance of it. Jesus Christ will do the rest.

Act 3: Restoration

So we come to Act 3; the title of this is *Restoration*. You know the story—how Mark returned to Paul and Barnabas; how Barnabas welcomed him eagerly, but Paul refused to have anything to do with him (surely if Jesus had been there, it would have been Barnabas's way not Paul's, He would have taken); how that unhappy dispute led to a quarrel and the quarrel to a parting, Barnabas going off with Mark, and Paul with Silas; how this splendid coward redeemed his reputation and proved himself a true hero of Christ, so that even Paul relented in the end and took him to his heart again. And when the great apostle lay waiting his death in Rome, it was of Mark that he kept thinking. "Take Mark," he wrote to Timothy, "and bring him with thee; for he is profitable to me for the ministry."

That is the familiar story. And this is the blessed and most glorious truth that it stands to announce to all who have ears to hear: the past can be blotted out. The heaviest and most shameful burden beneath which any soul in the world is staggering now is not too heavy for Jesus to deal with nor too shameful for Him to take up in His pierced, royal hands and cast finally away— so that the soul that has gone lame and limped under it for years will never set eyes on it again!

It would be a great thing—the Gospel of Jesus— even if it applied only to those who had fought the good fight and run the straight race all their lives. But blessed be God, it is more than that, far more. If the Christian preacher and evangelist has the gladdest and most thrilling task in all the world, it is because he has been authorized by God to proclaim the forgiveness of sins, the removing of their guilt and the shattering of their power. What is the Gospel? Hope for the hopeless, love for the unlovable, heroism for the most arrant coward, white shining robes for the most ragged, clean-hearted purity for the muddiest, inward peace and a great serenity for spirits torn and frantic with regret. There is a most moving scrap of conversation in George Macdonald's *Robert Falconer.*

"If I only knew that God was as good as that woman, I should be content."

"Then you don't believe that God is good?"

"I didn't say that, my boy. But to know that God was good and kind and fair—heartily, I mean, and not half-ways with ifs and buts. My boy, there would be nothing left to be miserable about."

Believe me, if you have once seen Jesus, as the men and women of the New Testament saw Him, there is nothing left to be miserable about. There is everything in the world to set you singing!

If I were to stand here and preach to you a limited gospel; if I were to tell you of a Christ who is the Lover of some elect, sky-blue souls who have never known the bitterness of self-despising and remorse, but not the Lover of all the world; if I were to suggest that there are depths of shame and humiliation and defeat from which the heights of heaven cannot be stormed; if I were to hedge God's loving-kindness around with ifs and buts and reservations and conditions—I should be preaching a lie. "Him that cometh to me I will in no wise cast out" (John 6:37). Was Jesus shocked when He saw them coming? Did Jesus ever turn around and say, "Ah, I did not mean you! I can go down deep to rescue the perishing, but not quite to such depths as that"? No, He saw them coming, lame and lost and lonely and sin-scarred and disillusioned and miserable, and He lifted up His eyes to heaven: "I thank You, Father, Lord of heaven and earth, that the Gospel of grace works even here! I thank You that You have sent Me to restore to these Your broken children the years that the locust has eaten." And He took them to His arms, God's bairns who had gotten hurt, and let them sob the whole sad story out. Then—"That is finished," He said, "behold, I make all things new." Do we today believe it? Take your own life, take the saddest recantation there has ever been, take the most locust-eaten year you can remember, take the thing that may be hiding God for you at this very moment. Lay that at Christ's feet. Say, "Lord, if Thou wilt ____!" And see if, for you, the ancient miracle is not renewed and the whole world filled with glory.

Act 4: Reparation

And so we end with Act 4 of Mark's story. We have watched his recantation and his remorse, and then his restoration. The title that this final act bears is *Reparation*. One thing only let me say in closing. How did Mark atone? How did he repair the damage he had done? He became an evangelist. He wrote a book. He gave the world a Life of Jesus, the first gospel to be written. We can be sure of this, that multitudes of people in those old, far-off days, who had never seen Jesus in the flesh, met Him in the pages of Mark's book, and entered—under the evangelist's guidance—upon the high road leading to salvation. And still today after all these years Mark is introducing men and women of every race and religion to Jesus and setting them face-to-face with the redeeming Son of God. That was his atonement. Was it not a glorious reparation?

What, then, of ourselves? We who have wounded Christ so often—is there any reparation we can offer? We cannot be evangelists like Mark, we say. It is not given to us to write gospels for the world to read. But think again! Is it not? The fact is there is not one of us here today who cannot compose a life of Jesus. You can write an evangel, not in books and documents, but in deeds and character. You can make people see Jesus. You can live in such a way that, even when you are not speaking about religion at all, you will be confronting souls with Christ—His ways, His spirit, His character—and making them feel the power and the beauty of the Son of God. And it may be that, all unknown to you, one soul here or another there will owe its very salvation to that gospel of yours; it may be that someone will rise from among the throngs around the judgment seat on the Last Day and pointing at you will cry: "There is the man to whom, under God, I owe everything! It was reading the Gospel of Christ in that man's life that redeemed me." And Jesus will turn to you with glad and grateful eyes. "Come, ye blessed of my Father, inherit the kingdom!" (Matt. 25:34).

Songs in Prison

George Campbell Morgan (1863–1945) was the son
of a British Baptist preacher and preached his first
sermon when he was thirteen years old. He had no
formal training for the ministry, but his tireless
devotion to the study of the Bible helped him to become
one of the leading Bible teachers of his day. Rejected
by the Methodists, he was ordained into the
Congregational ministry. He was associated with
Dwight L. Moody in the Northfield Bible conferences
and as an itinerant Bible teacher. He is best known as
the pastor of the Westminster Chapel, London (1904–
1917 and 1933–1945). During his second term there,
he had Dr. D. Martyn Lloyd-Jones as his associate.

Morgan published more than sixty books and
booklets, and his sermons are found in *The Westminster
Pulpit* (Hodder and Stoughton). This sermon is from
volume 9.

G. Campbell Morgan

6

SONGS IN PRISON

About midnight Paul and Silas were praying and singing hymns unto God, and the prisoners were listening to
them; and suddenly there was a great earthquake, so
that the foundations of the prison-house were shaken:
and immediately all the doors were opened; and every
one's bands were loosed (Acts 16:25–26 RV).

THIS IS AN ARRESTING and wonderful story, and the
more carefully it is considered the more the wonder
grows. At first we wonder at the singing. Then we
wonder so much at that which inspired the singing
that we should wonder more if these men had not sung.
At first we are amazed with the cheerfulness and
heroism of these men, and then we find out that their
singing was not abnormal but normal. It was not the
result of a transient emotion. It was the expression of
a constant experience of the soul.

Let us, then, first look at the picture presented by
these two verses; second, recognize the one central value
of the story in order that third and finally, we may
consider some of its particular teaching.

The Picture

These are the things that arrest attention. First the
men, Paul and Silas, then the circumstances in the midst
of which we see them, then their occupation in the midst
of the circumstances and finally, the issue of the story
as it is contained in all that remains of the chapter.

The men. Paul and Silas were Jews and were held in
contempt in Philippi because they were Jews, as is
most evident from this story. Yet, as emerges in the
course of the story, they were Roman citizens. But pre-
eminently they were Christians, the one an apostle
and the other a prophet.

Their ministry and their message necessarily challenged effete Judaism and paganism wherever they came. They were calling men to a new way of life both as to ideal and power. Consequently, wherever they went they created disturbances. "These that have turned the world upside down are come hither also!" (Acts 17:6). That is always the note of true Christianity. It always challenges effete religions and paganism. Organized Christianity that fails to make a disturbance is dead. It is equally true that they created love for themselves wherever they came. What tenderhearted affections fastened around this man Paul!

The circumstances. Now observe their circumstances at this time. "But about midnight . . ." That disjunctive sends us back as it suggests all that had gone before. They had been charged with sedition. They had been beaten with many stripes. Beating with rods was a terrible experience. When Paul was writing to the Corinthians, he referred to such beatings as among the things he had endured. "Thrice was I beaten with rods." It was physical brutality of the worst kind. Their backs were bruised and bleeding and unwashed. They were cast into the inner prison, some inner chamber or dungeon from which light was excluded and probably almost all air was shut out. The final barbarity was that their feet were made fast in the stocks. All that before the "But." Immediately following it are the words, "at midnight"! That accentuates everything. It accentuates the loneliness, the weariness, the suffering.

The occupation. We now come to that which is central: the occupation of these men. They were praying and singing hymns. This is not a description of two exercises. It does not mean that they were offering petitions and also singing hymns of praise. The word translated praying covers the whole ground of worship—asking for gifts, rendering of adoration, continued supplication, offering of thanksgiving. In this story the word *worship* is qualified by the word that follows. They were hymning the praises of God. The Greek word here employed is one that had long been reserved to represent the praises offered to heroes or gods or to the one God. The worship of these men was that of adoration. It was the expression of the gladness of their hearts. Two were gathered together in the Name and in the midst was the Lord, all unseen by the eyes of sense, unapprehended by any who were round about, undiscovered even after the jailer himself had come back to look at the prisoners. That Presence was the supreme sense of these men. They did not ask for anything, they gave. They were exercising their Christian priesthood on its highest level, which is not intercessory but eucharistic, the priesthood of thanksgiving. In the dungeon, in the darkness of the night, their feet fast in the stocks, their backs all bloody, they offered praises. They gave and their giving was the outcome of their gladness.

Immediately we ask, "What was there to make them glad?" I am inclined to answer the inquiry by saying that if we had asked them they probably would have said, "No, what is there to make us sad?"

The outcome. Finally, we must glance at the issue. The prisoners were listening! Here again a word arrests us. It indicates attentive listening. It is a word that is almost invariably employed for that listening which gives pleasure, the word used when men listened to perfect music and were charmed by its sounds, or when men listened to some oration that swept them away.

The Central Value

In all this story there is revealed that which is peculiarly Christian, the victory of the soul over all adverse circumstances and the transmutation of all opposing forces into allies of the soul. Think of some of the sayings of this man Paul who sang that night. He (in paraphrase) says, "Tribulation worketh patience, therefore rejoice in tribulation." He says, "Afflictions work a far more exceeding and eternal weight of glory, therefore we will rejoice in our afflictions." Yet again he says, "Godly sorrow worketh repentance." These are

all the things from which the soul of man shrinks—
tribulation, affliction, sorrow! These things are made
the allies of the soul, they work on behalf of the soul.
Out of tribulation comes patience which leads on to
confidence and hope of ultimate victory. Afflictions
which can be dismissed in the light of eternity as light
afflictions, which are but for a moment, are seen working out the weight of glory. Sorrows of the soul are
working toward the change of mind that means its trans-
formation into perfect harmony with the mind of Christ
Himself. This is the central value of the story. This is
the central truth concerning Christian experience.

What then was the secret of this experience in the
case of these men? It was the outcome of their knowledge of God. He was known as compelling all things to
work together for good to those who love Him. The
experience is not stoicism. The Christian man does not
say: "What cannot be cured must be endured." I am
afraid I have often said it, but when I have done so, it
has been because for the moment I have forgotten my
Christianity. To say that what cannot be cured must
be endured is paganism. It is wonderful that paganism
ever climbed to that height. It is a great attitude, it is
heroic up to a certain point, but it is not Christianity.
Christianity does not say what cannot be cured must
be endured; it says, rather, that these things must be
endured because they are part of the cure. These things
are to be cheerfully borne because they have the strange
and mystic power to make whole and strong and so to
lead on to victory and the final glory. Christianity is
never the dour pessimism that submits. Christianity
is the cheerful optimism that cooperates with the process because it sees that through suffering and weakness, joy and triumph must come. That always and
only results from a clear vision of God. Wherever this
clear vision of God comes to the soul through Christ—
through whom alone it can come—there follows the
ending of bondage to all secondary causes, and the
sense of relationship to the primary and final cause is
supreme.

Two men were in Philippi, in prison, in the inner prison, in the stocks, in suffering, in sorrow! All true, but the final thing is not said. They were in God! Their supreme consciousness was not that of the prison or the stocks or the pain, but of God. They were not callous or indifferent; pain was pain to them, confinement was confinement, loneliness was loneliness; but they realized how all these things were yet held in the grasp of the King of the perfect order, whom they knew as their Lord and Master, and, consequently, they sang praises. They did not ask for anything, not even for an earthquake. They gave Him praises. That is Christianity. Because of this vision of God and because of this sense of the soul, the experiences which otherwise would have depressed and led to despair became wings of hope, the inspiration of song.

All this took place at midnight! That accentuates all the difficulty, the loneliness and weariness and pain. Yet the phrase is not really "at midnight." This very slight alteration in the Revised Version is not to be passed over lightly. "About midnight!" To these men midnight was not a definite moment at all. Midnight is never a stopping place. It is coming, and lo! it is gone before we know it. Time is transfigured. There is no long, deadly moment with all the agony of eternity pressed into it to these men. They are traveling, and they are traveling in the spirit of the hymn:

> We're marching through Immanuel's ground
> To fairer worlds on high.

Through Immanuel's land, not to Immanuel's land, but through it. John Bunyan puts the river his pilgrim had to cross in Immanuel's land. The pilgrim did not cross the river to reach Immanuel's land; the river was in it and before he knew it, he had passed the river. So to these men all these things were in Immanuel's land. Midnight, that deadly hour, that most terrible hour, wherein some people seem forever to dwell; anticipation of it makes it a perpetual presence and the memory of it an abounding agony. But for these men there was no such actual time. It was about midnight, and then they sang, and they sang praises to God.

The Teaching

What then are the things of value here for us? In attempting to answer this inquiry let us keep our mind upon these men. First, we learn that *men who sing while they suffer are men who have learned the profound secret that suffering is the method by which joy is perfected.* That declaration is limited by human history as we know it. I am not prepared to say that we can make a statement like that and apply it to the whole universe of God. It is conceivable that there may be abounding joys in God's great universe that have never been reached through suffering. I cannot tell. I do not know. I do not ask to know. I am dealing with humanity as the result of our own experience and in the light of the biblical unveiling. Suffering is always the method by which joy is perfected. In the midst of the Paschal Discourses our Lord said: "Your sorrow shall be turned into joy" (John 16:20). That is an entirely different thing from saying that your sorrow shall be exchanged for joy. Without desiring for a moment to be censorious in criticism, yet it is true that half our hymns suggest that we should look on to heaven where we shall find a joy that is a compensation for the sorrows of life.

There is truth in that view, but it does not get to the heart of the Christian revelation. The truth is that all the ultimate joys of the heavenly state are joys that have come out of the agonies of the earthly tribulation. Is that a startling thing to say? Then listen to these most revealing words: "who for the joy that was set before him endured the cross, despising shame" (Heb. 12:2). With infinite reverence I say that He had never reached that joy save through His sorrows. That which was wrought out in the experience of our Lord on our behalf is a revelation of what all this pain means—this abounding, palpitating, poignant agony. Your sorrow shall be turned into joy. Again and again we have glimpses of it, outworking into the present of immediate experience.

Look back over the years. There they are, travel-worn years; much of light is upon them but much of darkness also; many days of triumph, marching with the band playing and the flags flying and many days of disaster and defeat. Already you know that the greatest things of life have come not out of the sunlit days, but out of the darkened hours. Your sorrow has already been turned into joy. When your sorrow, which seemed unendurable at the hour, blossomed with beauty, your sorrow was turned into joy. Christianity as an experience is the ability to know that this will be so even while the agony is upon us, and so we are able to sing in the midst of it. Men who sing while they suffer are men who have learned the profound secret that suffering is the method by which joy is perfected in human life and human history.

But again, *men who sing in prison are men who cannot be imprisoned*. It was impossible to imprison Paul and Silas. But they were imprisoned. They could be shown in that prison, in that inner chamber, with their feet fast in the stocks. Ah, but they were not imprisoned. Fellowship with God is the franchise of eternity. You may put these men within your stone walls, you may make their feet fast in the wood of your brutal stocks, but they are not there. They are sitting with Christ in the heavenly places. They are ranging themselves with the living ones. They are swinging the censers of their heavenly priesthood in high and holy places. As to bodily presence, they are there in the prison, but as to spiritual essence they are with God. Men who sing in prison are men who cannot be imprisoned.

Therefore we may add: *men who sing at midnight are citizens of that city of which it is said they need no light of sun or moon, for the Lord and the Lamb are the light of it*. But they are in Philippi! Yes, as to bodily presence but not as to spiritual experience. Abraham left Ur of the Chaldees to find a city but never found it. He died without seeing it. Those who have followed in his steps have still been seeking it. It has never been found. It is not found yet. But it is clearly seen; it will be built; it will be established. Abraham lived in it though he never saw it; he walked its streets though it was never built; he held communion with its inhabitants though he never reached it. Paul and Silas, where are you living just now? In Philippi? No, in the city of God! In the city of God there is no night. These men were children of light, they were stars of the morning, and the morning stars sang together long ago, and they will sing together through all earth's midnight until the last shadow is melted. Men who sing at midnight are citizens of the city in which there is no night.

And finally, *men who sing when their work is stopped are men whose work is never stopped.*

They have put Paul in prison. His beloved work is stopped. He cannot preach in prison. But they sing praises, and the prisoners are listening. A man who can sing in prison is a man whose work is never done. When the missionary journey has to be abandoned and the preaching services are all canceled and there is nothing more to do, he will sing and the prisoners will hear his singing. The singing of a prisoner is a message to prisoners and they will listen. I cannot go any further. I do not know what happened to those prisoners afterward. If you will allow the speculation, I believe that some of them were brought to Jesus Christ as the result of that singing. Cancel that if you do not agree. At least one man was won for Christ: the hard, brutalized man who had been able to put these men in the stocks in the inner prison and leave them all bleeding from the rods and faint with loss of blood. He had left them and gone to sleep. He was asleep. If you want to know how brutalized he was, get that upon your heart. What is the next thing we see him doing? Washing their stripes, his whole nature revolutionized, his whole being completely changed with a suddenness equal to that of the earthquake that shook the prison to its foundations. He is washing their stripes; he is putting food before them. Men who sing in prison when their work is stopped are given to see that their work is never stopped; it runs on through bondage to liberty, and the Gospel is preached anew.

All I have so far said has had to do with one verse of my text. There is another verse. "Suddenly there was a great earthquake, so that the foundations of the prison-house were shaken: and immediately all the doors were opened; and everyone's bands were loosed." That was very wonderful, but we will not dwell upon it. I made it part of the text in order to say that it does not matter. It does not at all affect our story. It does not rob from it; it does not add to it. The glory of our consideration is in the other verse. That earthquake does not always come. We shall miss a great deal if we imagine that when we are in prison and sing there will be an earthquake. Prison doors may not be opened at all. Thousands have been left in prison and died there, but they sang, and they sang through until they joined the new song on the other side. That earthquake does not matter. Do not let us fix our minds upon the earthquake. Probably we shall never have a deliverance like that. That is not the point of the story at all.

Two or three years passed away and Paul was in prison in Rome, and then he wrote to these very people, to this jailer and these Philippians. Read his letter, the letter he wrote to these very people from another prison. It is a song from beginning to end. He was still singing, and there was no earthquake. But probably he was liberated. Yes, I agree. Possibly he expected to be liberated. Indeed, he surely did as that letter shows. But he was not singing because he was to be liberated. Read the letter through, and you will see that the inspiration of his song was not the expectation of deliverance. It was the realization while he was in prison of the fact that he was a prisoner of Jesus Christ. That is the secret of the singing in the Philippian letter. That sense of relationship to Jesus Christ transfigured everything else. The chain? He looked at it, but it flashed with light. He was the prisoner of Jesus Christ.

Let us go on. Presently, he was in prison again, and he was never coming out, and he knew it. His last writing was the letter of a man in prison never to escape. He knew it perfectly well. Things had not gone well with him in the first part of his trial, and he was assured that the issue of the second part of it would be death. How then did he write? What is he doing? Listen to him for a moment:

> For I am already being offered, and the time of my departure is come. I have fought the good fight, I have finished the course, I have kept the faith: henceforth there is laid up for me the crown of righteousness, which the Lord, the righteous judge, shall give to me at that day: and not only to me, but also to all them that have loved his appearing (2 Tim. 4:6–8).

He was singing still; still an anthem, still a paean of praise! They were very dark days. Listen!

> Do thy diligence to come shortly unto me: for Demas forsook me, having loved this present world, and went to Thessalonica; Crescens to Galatia, Titus to Dalmatia. Only Luke is with me. Take Mark, and bring him with thee: for he is useful to me for ministering. But Tychicus I sent to Ephesus. [It is colder here.] The cloke that I left at Troas with Carpus, bring when thou comest, and the books, especially the parchments. Alexander the coppersmith did me much evil (vv. 9–14).

Do you see the conflicting circumstances? Was he singing now?

> At my first defence no one took my part, but all forsook me: may it not be laid to their account. But the Lord stood by me, and strengthened me; that through me the message might be fully proclaimed, and that all the Gentiles might hear: and I was delivered out of the mouth of the lion. The Lord will deliver me from every evil work, and will save me unto His heavenly kingdom: to whom be glory forever and ever (vv. 16–18).

He was singing still. Ah yes! and the singing that we have listened to in Philippi was before the earthquake. He had no idea that the earthquake was coming. He did not sing because he was to be let out of prison. He sang because prison did not matter.

> Your harps, ye trembling saints,
>   Down from the willows take;
> Loud to the praise of Love divine,
>   Bid every string awake.
>
> His Grace will to the end,
>   Stronger and brighter shine;
> Nor present things, nor things to come,
>   Shall quench the spark divine.
>
> When we in darkness walk,
>   Nor feel the heavenly flame,
> Then is the time to trust our God,
>   And rest upon His Name.
>
> Blest is the man, O God,
>   That stays himself on Thee!
> Who wait for Thy salvation, Lord,
>   Shall Thy salvation see!

Taking the Hazard

John Henry Jowett (1864–1923) was known as "the greatest preacher in the English-speaking world." He was born in Yorkshire, England. He was ordained into the Congregational ministry, and his second pastorate was at the famous Carr's Lane Church, Birmingham, where he followed the eminent Dr. Robert W. Dale. From 1911 to 1918, he pastored the Fifth Avenue Presbyterian Church, New York City; from 1918 to 1923, he ministered at Westminster Chapel, London, succeeding G. Campbell Morgan. He wrote many books of devotional messages and sermons.

This message is taken from *God—Our Contemporary*, published by Fleming H. Revell in 1922.

John Henry Jowett

7

TAKING THE HAZARD

Our beloved Barnabas and Paul, men that have hazarded their lives for the name of our Lord Jesus Christ (Acts 15:25–26).

HERE IS SOMETHING VERY delightful in finding these two men bracketed together in a common roll of honor. Both of them are hazarding their lives for the Lord Jesus Christ, and the two men are strikingly dissimilar. Their characters are distinguished by a common loyalty, but their characteristics are strangely different. They are like two musical notes, both of them absolutely in tune, but expressing quite different qualities of sound. In many ways it would be difficult to find two men more unlike than Barnabas and Paul, yet they both gambled with their lives and put them in hazard in their fidelity to the Lord Jesus Christ.

I am not surprised to have this news concerning the apostle Paul. I do not wonder that he sprang into the thick of dangers as naturally as the stormy petrel lifts her wings at the call of the tempest. For Paul was a born warrior. He was a "bonny fighter"! If a menace arose, or any threat was in the air, his spirit was refreshed. Where is there a record of any antagonist appearing where we find Paul nervously sulking away to his tent? The way of difficulty was always his favorite road. He loved the battle and the breeze. He reveled in close grips with stern wrestlers, and that day was always most welcome that promised a struggle from which he could extort the prize of victory. I do not, therefore, wonder that this man hazarded his life for the Lord Jesus, that he flung himself into the midst of a crowd of adversaries and that he staked everything upon his triumph.

But Barnabas was a very different type of man. I imagine him to be the kind of a man whom we describe as a home-bird. He was more a man of the fireside. He was gentle, companionable, sweet. He was pastoral where Paul was militant. He was the "son of consolation" while Paul was a man of war. Where Paul would carry a sword, in readiness for an adversary, Barnabas would carry a wallet, filled with oil and wine, in readiness for any traveler whom he might find robbed and beaten on the road. He was a peacemaker, and he was great in the ministry of reconciliation. When Paul would have dismissed a man for cowardice, Barnabas would give him another chance. And so he was greatly distinguished by the softer and more genial virtues. I would not compare him to some splendid cedar, with branches like an athlete's limbs, joyfully contending with tempests on the heights of Lebanon; he was more like a domesticated olive tree, quiet and gentle, laden with fruit, but having its home in the sheltered vale. It was the difference between Jonathan and David, between John and Peter, between Ridley and Latimer, between Gordon and Kitchener. And yet we are told that Barnabas also, the man of pacific virtues, the man who was clothed in softer and more retiring moods, heard the trumpet call of the hour and hazarded his life for the name of the Lord Jesus Christ. The olive tree revealed the strength and fiber of the cedar. Barnabas and Paul united their dissimilarities in a common and glorious venture. They hazarded all they had. They gambled everything for Christ.

Now, what was it that prompted them to take the hazard? It was the name of the Lord Jesus. They spoke of the name where the name carried their fate. Our circumstances are now so different that we have to deliberately enlist the imagination and the historic sense to create the scene and to give reality and life to the record. I can anywhere proclaim the name of the Lord Jesus, and the name is my security rather than my offense. I exalt it here in this house of prayer, and there is none to make me afraid. I can announce the name of Jesus like a herald in any open square or on any village green in the kingdom, and no menace would darken my steps. The fact of the matter is this—in this our land the name of Jesus has no religious rival, and when we "hail the power of Jesus' name," there is no contendent for His throne. You can trudge from coast to border, and you can mark the milestones of your pilgrimage by the proclamation of the name of Christ, and never in the entire journey will your life be in hazard or your safety in peril or your comfort broken. To merely declare the name of Christ in our day does not in any way recall the circumstances of the early church.

For, look you, take an example. When Paul went to Ephesus to proclaim the name of Jesus there was another name there before Him. "Great is Diana of the Ephesians" (Acts 19:28)! There was a rival on the field. The rival was mighty and predominant. The rival was revered. "Great is Diana of the Ephesians" (Acts 19:34)! And to go into the city of Ephesus and stand up in some public square and proclaim, "Great is Jesus of Nazareth," was to carry your life in your hands, to arouse the enmity of rivalry, to stir the fires of pride and prejudice, and to enlist against you all the fiercest hatreds of religious passion. To say the name of Jesus where everybody else was saying the name of Diana was to gamble with your safety and to put your life in hazard. And if some Ephesian, learning the name from you, went along his old ways singing something like this, "How sweet the name of Jesus sounds," or this, "Jesus, the name to sinners dear," or this, "The name above every name," or this, "Jesus, the name high over all," what then? What about Diana? What had that man to face? The pointing finger was outstretched, and the menacing cry was raised, Yah! Anti-Diana! Anti-Diana! Pro-Nazarene! If we would know what he had to face we must recreate and recall the use of phrases like Pro-Boer, or Pro-German, or Anti-Patriotic, or Anti-Loyalist, or any other circumstance where some hoary and accepted tradition has opened the armory of its terrors and marched against anyone who has questioned its right and authority. In such remembrance we shall recover something of the mood and temperature of those early days. Well, then, in face of all this menace in Ephesus, how did the apostles fare? Let us hear again the simple record, They magnified the name of the Lord Jesus; they hazarded their lives for the name of our Lord Jesus Christ.

It is just here that we may see the intervening years between their day and ours melt away, and we may feel the essential kinship between Ephesus and London. There is now little or no hazard in proclaiming the name of Jesus. There is no Diana within our shores to awaken battle. But loyalty to the name of Jesus is as provocative in our day as it was nineteen hundred years ago. There may be no exalted, tinseled monarch who is jealous of our fine gold, but you cannot maintain your loyalty to Christ without facing the menace of mammon, or the irritation of fashion, or the heavy inertia of tradition, or the sleepless antagonism of the world, the flesh, and the Devil. Diana has vanished! I said Jesus had no rivals in Britain, and yet these are fierce contenders for her power. The way of Christian loyalty is on that road, the road of open venture. And the all-determining question is this—How far will we go in our religious devotion? What is the extent of our stake? How much will we hazard for Christ? Paul and Barnabas hazarded their *lives* for the name of the Lord Jesus Christ.

For, after all, the real test of the value of our religion is found in the stake that we are willing to wager in the name of our Lord. In one of his books Donald Hankey has a very arresting phrase. It is this: "True religion is betting one's life that there is a God." I want you to notice the nature of the bet. You don't bet your word that there is a God. You don't bet ten minutes or a quarter of an hour a day that there is a God. You don't hazard three pence a week that there is a God. You bet your life on it. That is the stake. "True religion is betting one's life that there is a God." I say that

Donald Hankey's phrase is very arresting and very quickening, but there is not enough life and color in it for me. I wonder how the apostle Paul would recast and remint the phrase. Most assuredly he would so remold it as to make room for Christ. I wonder if this might be anything like the refashioning: The true Christian religion is betting one's life that Jesus is the Son of God and the Savior of the world and hazarding everything for the honor of His friendship. At any rate, however we may phrase the form of the venture, we may surely say that the Scriptures and Donald Hankey's statement agree in this, that vital religion implies the element of hazard, of speculation, of splendid gamble, and that where there is no risk the so-called venture is dead.

Well, if that be so, we have a ready measure for testing the reality and value of our religious professions. We need not begin with prolonged investigation into the length and details of our theological creed. I have known men and women with a creed as long as your arm, but they had no more spirit of venture than a limpet. Their theology is like a mountain, but they have not the courage of a mouse. Our jealousy for orthodoxy is no proof at all of the value of our faith. What do we hazard for it? The measure of the hazard reveals the vitality of our faith, and nothing else reveals it. It is not revealed by our controversial ardor. It is not revealed by our stern guardianship of orthodox spoils. It is not revealed by the scrupulous regularity of our attendance at church and worship. No, all these may mean nothing at all. What do we hazard for Christ? What have we staked on the venture? How much have we bet that He is alive and King? Two pence a week— or our lives? That is the test. Paul and Barnabas hazarded their lives for the Lord Jesus Christ. They staked everything on Him.

Now the New Testament teaches that the heart of faith is venture. If you will study the eleventh chapter of the letter to the Hebrews, that wonderful chapter where the heroes and heroines of faith are honored and commemorated as in the gathered memorials of some venerable cathedral—if you will study the shining legends of that chapter you will find that every instance reveals a vista of venture. Some man or woman is taking a hazard. Every memorial begins with the majestic prelude, "By faith, so and so . . .," and the sentence goes on to describe a splendid risk. Every emblazoned record preserves the renown of some man or woman who staked everything on the faithfulness of God. You pass from one to another, and they are all the stories of hazardous exploits. They are very dissimilar. In one instance a man is venturously putting himself at the head of a mass movement of his fellow countrymen, and he is leading them out of agelong bondage. In another instance a woman puts a bit of scarlet thread in a window and risks her life in the venture. Yes, they are very dissimilar. The roads are very different, but they are all alike in the display of a common venture. And therefore do I say, on the authority of the Word of God, that there is no true faith without venture. Merely to hug a creed and to take no risk is no more faith than to hug a timetable is to take a journey.

Look at it from another angle for a moment. Let us ask this question—What faculties are involved in the work of faith? Reason? Surely. Conscience? Yes, surely. Imagination? Yes. Emotion? Yes, and no; possibly, but not necessarily. You may have faith without emotion, as some bulbs open out their hidden glory without water, absorbing from the atmosphere the scanty moisture that they need. You have all these other faculties at work, and yet faith may still be dead. Reason, conscience, imagination may all be present, and yet there may be no splendid ventures of movement in the life. Reason may perfect her logical steps and processes. Conscience may become incandescent. Imagination may cherish nobler ideals. Emotion may awake in sacred and chivalrous desire. You may have all these, yet you may not have the faith that will entitle you to be honored in the ranks of those whose glories are recounted in the letter to the Hebrews.

In those shining records you see not only reason in logical movement and conscience surveying larger moral issues and imagination scanning the outlines of new worlds and emotion expressing itself in penitential word and tears, you see more than these. In the faith of these men and women it is *life* itself that is moving, and it is moving in glorious hazard and venture. Reason is there and conscience and imagination, but all these are vitalized by the vitalizing companionship of the will, and it is the will moving in venturesome journeys.

If you have reason and conscience and imagination without the will, it is like having three finely upholstered railway carriages, but no engine. They are all right to stand in a station, and you can rest and sleep in them, but they are no use for a journey. Add the engine, and the whole is in movement, and you can go to the ends of the earth! Reason, conscience, imagination—now add will, a venturesome will! It is in the valorous movement of the will, staking everything upon her venture, that life is displayed in the vitality and regality of faith.

These heroes and heroines are all in movement, and it is always the movement of hazard and gamble: They "stopped the mouths of lions, quenched the violence of fire, escaped the edge of the sword, . . . turned to flight the armies of the aliens. . . . Others had trial of cruel mockings and scourgings, yea, moreover of bonds and imprisonment: They were stoned, they were sawn asunder, were tempted, were slain with the sword" (Heb. 11:33–37). What wealth of hazard here! What prodigality of venture! And what is their venture? It is all hidden in this phrase, "By faith"! A risking will converts a passive belief into an active faith. Without hazard there is no faith. Faith without works is dead. Paul and Barnabas hazarded their lives for the name of the Lord Jesus Christ. They gambled everything on His truth and grace.

And now let me add this word in conclusion. A religion without hazard is a religion that makes no discoveries. Nothing ventured, nothing won! That is the teaching of the world on other roads of experience. It is also the teaching of the Word of God. Nothing ventured, nothing won! Our hazards are methods of exploration, and they are the measures of our findings. No stakes, no winnings! Splendid gambling, splendid gains! What sort of gains? Read what Jesus Christ says about them. What sort of gains? Read what the apostle Paul says about them. You may possibly remain as poor as a struggling village carpenter, but you will assuredly share the riches of the Son of God. Aye, but there is something even better than that. In the common sort of gambling no one grows richer except the winner. But where a man or woman hazards his or her life on the Christ everybody shares the gains. All men are better when any man sides with God. He sweetens the world for everybody else. Every noble venture brings heaven into the common road and makes it fragrant with the perfume of divine truth and grace.

How much shall we put into our religion? What shall we hazard? How much money shall we put into it? Shall it be less than we put on our backs, less than we put into the theaters? How much faculty shall we put into it? How much glory and strength? Shall we toy with it or shall we gamble our lives in the business? What shall we put into it ?

> Were the whole realm of nature mine,
>   That were a present far too small:
> Love so amazing, so divine,
>   Demands my soul, my life, my all.

NOTES

Saint Paul at Ephesus

Henry Parry Liddon (1829–1890) belonged to the High Church school of the Anglican Church. Ordained in 1853, he served in two brief pastorates and as vice principal of a school. He moved to Oxford and there preached to large crowds at Saint Mary's and Christ Church. He is perhaps best known for his Bampton Lectures, *The Divinity of Our Lord and Savior Jesus Christ.* From 1870 to his death, he was canon of Saint Paul's Cathedral, London, which he sought to make into an Anglican preaching center to rival Charles Spurgeon's Metropolitan Tabernacle.

This sermon is taken from *Sermons by Rev. H. P. Liddon*, published by Swan Sonnenschein & Co., London, 1892.

Henry Parry Liddon

8

SAINT PAUL AT EPHESUS

For I will not see you now by the way; but I trust to tarry awhile with you, if the Lord permit. But I will tarry at Ephesus until Pentecost. For a great door and effectual is opened unto me, and there are many adversaries (1 Corinthians 16:7–9).

IT IS FROM INCIDENTAL passages like these in the apostle's writings that we obtain the deepest and most vivid insight into the writer's mind and character. Among uninspired writings it is not in formal depositions or official documents that that which constitutes personal character and life makes itself felt. Few persons, I apprehend, would be found disposed to endorse the paradox of a modern historian who tells us that the character of King Henry VIII is to be studied most advantageously in the preambles to his Acts of Parliament. The great charm of private correspondence, and the one reason that can in many cases justify or explain its publication, is that it is a revelation of human character. In their public capacities, two men of profoundly different character will say exactly the same thing and in the same way, the truth being that for the time all personal characteristics are dropped. It is the office or the circumstances or the necessities of the case that really speaks. It is not the man. In private correspondence, however, you see a man as he is. He writes what he thinks and what he feels from moment to moment. His enthusiasm, his impulses, his hopes, his fears, his attractions and repulsions are all represented by turns. They are uttered without design, or, more correctly perhaps, they escape from him in spite of himself. As you read you feel that you are in contact not with a formal and systematic composition, but with the soul of the writer—the soul in all its strength or in all its weakness, in all its thoroughness or all its inconsistency, in all its inertness or all its energy and resolution.

Now, it is one of the greatest attractions of Saint Paul's epistles that while they embody the great and essential doctrines of Christianity, they also abound in those incidental passages or elements that keep the character and figure of the writer continually before us. It is this that enables us all, but especially those of us who have succeeded in whatever measure or degree in furthering the apostle's work, to feel toward him as a personal friend, just as if eighteen centuries did not divide him from us; just as though we had him now here with us in London or Southwark, or we were back with him in one of the ancient cities of the Levant.

The passage before us well illustrates this observation. The apostle reveals his intention to remain in Ephesus until the Pentecost and thus shows to us a feature of his character well worthy of our consideration upon an occasion like the present. "But I will tarry at Ephesus until Pentecost. For a great door and effectual is opened unto me, and there are many adversaries."

Now here we have, first of all, an announcement of the decision the apostle had come to, and secondly, the reasons upon which that decision is based. In the determination of the apostle to remain at Ephesus until Pentecost, let us recognize first, the apostle's power or faculty of making up his mind in the face of strong counterbalancing motives. There was enough in the nature and circumstances of his life at this time to have made him desirous to leave Ephesus at a moment's notice when he wrote these lines. It would have been easy to frame a long catalog of reasons, each of which would have exercised over the mind of any man but such as the apostle Paul an almost commanding power.

Paul's Announcement

Saint Paul, as has been pointed out by a recent critic, had come back to Ephesus from a visit to Corinth, and he had arrived in low spirits. He had gone on account of the state of the Corinthian church, of which he had heard a bad account, but had found matters worse than he expected. In an epistle that has been lost to us, he had ordered that certain members whose conduct had been the cause of great public scandal should be excluded from the church. The church, too, was divided by the bitterest party spirit. That portion of the Christian community which desired to retain as much as possible of the old law of the Jews was attempting to undermine the teaching of Saint Paul, whom they considered too enthusiastic. Others, although he was a pupil of Gamaliel, could discover nothing interesting in his teaching. Another party refused allegiance in several matters of church government, while a fourth section denied all connection with his party and applied to a higher name for a head, thus showing that they had carried party spirit to a greater pitch of narrowness than the rest. There was also a party—whether known to the apostle or not it is impossible to say— that denied the resurrection of the dead and regarded the Gospel teaching as a kind of refined Epicureanism. This party, though professing to be connected with the church, lived in open opposition to her teachings. The law courts, again, were constantly occupied with suits brought against one another by litigious members of the community; the gifts of the Holy Spirit were made into occasions for the exhibition of the pettiest of personal disputes; Christian women, forgetting their higher instincts and the customs of their country that embodied those instincts, came forward unveiled to make public speeches in the assemblies of the church. It seemed as if the Greek character and nature, brilliant but paradoxical, had carried all its resources of finesse and intrigue, all its genius for controversy, and all its profound distaste for personal improvement into the heart of the church at Corinth.

The apostle may well have felt that he ought to be on the spot where there was so much mischief to prevent and to cure. It must have cost him much pain, with all his burning sympathy for his Master's cause, to have set aside the claims of Corinth even for six weeks. But still he did, though he must have known that there was one voice to which all the church there would listen, one heart to which all would sooner or later respond, one will to which all would bend. His presence at Corinth was of the first necessity, but there was a higher necessity for him to be elsewhere, so he struck the balance at once. Indecision may be a characteristic of a weak mind, but in this case the apostle looked at the matter in the practical way everyone who has a mission for advancing the religion of Christ must do. For we have to work for a cause that can never be universally popular and in the presence of an enemy who never sleeps and by whom any errors we may commit are certainly and immediately taken advantage of.

There is no doubt that prompt decision as to the right course is at times a matter of the greatest difficulty, but we who serve Christ Jesus our Lord in a sense different from other men dare not abdicate the duty—the great duty—of decision. If rash resolution be wrong, the absence of all resolution is not right. The man asserts his innate manhood, the Christian puts forth the power of the indwelling Christ when, feeling that God's eye is upon him and that he shall one day stand before the great judgment seat, he makes up his mind upon this matter of great importance; when, taking all his passions, feelings, hopes, fears, ambitions, and enthusiasms well in hand, he proclaims from amidst the very chaos of tumult within him the sentence of that sovereign faculty of his race, the sentence of his will, of a will placed under the guidance of a well-instructed conscience. Saint Paul has told us in one place, "I find then a law, that, when I would do good, evil is present with me. For I delight in the law of God after the inward man: but I see another law in my members, warring against the law of my mind, and bringing me into captivity to the law of sin which is in my members" (Rom. 7:21–23). But here we see him not hesitating, not irresolutely parleying with countervailing motives, still less resistlessly yielding the mastery to impulse, but forming his purpose calmly. His resolution is formed, but yet he has it well in hand. He knows how far to let the reins go and when to draw them in, and he says, "I will tarry at Ephesus until Pentecost."

Paul's Reasons

Now, upon what reasons was this decision founded? Upon two; of these the first is *the greatness of the opportunity* afforded by the approaching festival of Pentecost at Ephesus. Saint Paul, in his vivid and expressive way, calls the opportunity a "door," by which he hoped might enter all those who were nearest and dearest to his heart. No, he intensifies his metaphor almost at the risk of destroying it, for he tells us it is not only a "great door" but that it is "effectual," as if the whole act were instinct with his motive, as though it were impossible for the apostle not to endeavor to make the most of every opportunity. It had not always been thus at Ephesus. Saint Paul must have heard much about the fervid teaching of the eloquent Apollos, following upon the labors of Aquila and Priscilla, but yet it must have cheered his heart to have the prospect of baptizing more converts to the influence of the Holy Spirit. Accordingly, he resolved to stay at Ephesus, and he made the Jewish synagogue in that city the starting point of his activity. Saturday after Saturday, for three months, he went there preaching and arguing—holding what in these times we should call a series of "conferences"—upon the religion of God and salvation through Jesus Christ. As a pupil of Gamaliel he knew well the way to approach the hearts of his countrymen. He knew that the kingdom of the Messiah, as shadowed forth in the sacred writings, was a very different thing from the hard, dry, political institution, the idea of which was then popular among the Jews.

But though Saint Paul preached to ears which did not mean to be convinced and though the Ephesians would not do justice to the preacher, they could not afford to treat him with contempt. Accordingly, his preaching was denounced with insult. It was then that he determined to separate himself from the main body of the Jews, and thenceforth he taught his disciples in one of those side wings or buildings usually attached to the public baths and gymnasiums and that was frequented by Tyrannus, who was probably a teacher of rhetoric. There he was, day by day, sometimes speaking to pagans and sometimes to his own countrymen, upon the nature and claims of the Gospel. There would be found men from all parts of Asia to which the news of Saint Paul's teaching had penetrated, and there would be discussed the miracles and remarkable events that we read of in the Acts of the Apostles—the public discomfiture of the seven sons of the priest Sceva, who attempted to make use of the sacred name of Jesus in their incantations; the burning of the costly books filled with the recipes of the magicians. It was felt, in fact, that a new moral force had gone forth from that spot, and society was fermenting all around.

No one would have felt this more than Saint Paul. "A great door and effectual," he says, "is opened unto me." The whole mass of Jewish thought was heaving with agitation before his mind's eye. Men were asking all around him, What was really truth? What was worth living for? What was worth dying for?—if there were any such thing at all? There was a wish to base life, if it could be done, upon a moral rock of some kind. There was an impatience of all that was not real. These effects were not the Gospel itself but they were preparatory for the Gospel. The soil had to be broken up by these means before the heavenly seed could be sown with any probability of growth.

It is no slight part of our responsibility to make the most of every opportunity for doing our Master's work. It is not too much to say that every one of us has some such opportunities sooner or later. We may have perhaps to work at first without encouragement in the synagogue, but a school of Tyrannus comes to all of us at last. To fail to make the most of the opportunity, when it does come, is possible enough from our human weakness; but to fail to try, to make no effort to comprehend that the opportunity has arrived, to be content to glide down the stream of life as though there was nothing particular in it, nothing that would have any bearing upon our highest good or that of others, implies some grave disease in our moral and spiritual constitution, if not, indeed, that deadly apathy for which the stern realities of spiritual life and death have no meaning. Saint Paul, according to all testimony, was constantly saying or doing something, and that he was constantly succeeding was for this among other reasons, that he was always alive to opportunities of success.

The second reason given by the apostle for remaining at Ephesus until the Pentecost was *the difficulty of the situation*. "There," said he, "are many adversaries." To begin with, there were, of course, the Jews of the synagogue, who would have forgotten the circumstances which had led to the secession of the school of Tyrannus. Then there would be the mass of turbulent spirits reduced to something like decorum by military force, but always ready to break out again, and who could command the services of some powerful adherents. Already the apostle discerned the coming storm. He did not suppose for a moment that the religion of the Crucified One could make itself a home with that joyous, pleasure-seeking, easy-tempered, and superstitious population without a struggle. Sooner or later it must come into conflict with the classes who were deeply concerned in abasing it even to the death.

There were at this time a large number of skilled workmen who lived by making miniature copies of the inner shrine of the temple of Diana. These copies were purchased by visitors and placed as ornaments upon the tables or elsewhere in the interior of the houses of the wealthy. All these men were of course interested in preventing the triumph of Christianity. They were bound to the worship of Diana by the double tie of old association and commercial enterprise, and such a combination in favor of any very good or very bad system is, as a matter of experience, always exceedingly strong. Then, again, the working men throughout Asia Minor, as shown by some inscriptions that have been only lately discovered, were almost universally enrolled in guilds or trades unions so that when the interests of any particular trade were assailed, nothing was easier than to arouse opposition of a very serious kind.

Saint Paul, well knowing of the existence of fraternities of men like Demetrius, must have had reason to anticipate such scenes as the riot at the theater being at least very probable. But the thought of coming difficulties acted only as a stimulus to him to take advantage of this opportunity for Christian work and Christian virtue. For what does virtue mean but strong moral force put forward under difficulties, in accordance with the rule of right, and put forward more frequently when surrounded by such difficulties. In fact, difficulty is necessary to the full development of virtue, just as the soft atmosphere of unimpeded success fosters slowly, yet surely, moral weakness and moral decay.

Therefore it was that Saint Paul looked at these "many adversaries" not only as being no drawback, but as a positive attraction. They raised within him not any mere spirit of natural brute combativeness, but that spiritualized military temper which he tells us in his epistle to the Ephesians is one great characteristic of the true Christian. He was a soldier by profession and had become a good soldier of Jesus Christ. He therefore felt that it was a good thing to be on the field of battle and taking note of the strength of the enemy. For every opponent there was a possible convert; every opponent there was at any rate in the last resort but an impotent antagonist. "Who shall separate us," he cries at last, "from the love of Christ? shall tribulation, or distress, or persecution, or famine, or nakedness, or peril, or sword? . . . Nay, in all these things we are more than conquerors through him that loved us. For I am persuaded, that neither death, nor life, nor angels, nor principalities, nor powers, nor things present, nor things to come, nor height, nor depth, nor any other creature, shall be able to separate us from the love of God, which is in Christ Jesus our Lord" (Rom. 8:35–39).

But, my brethren, this solemn occasion speaks for itself. Words are often out of place when men's hearts are full, when there is much that flits before the eye of the soul which words cannot compass. Those of us who are here this morning as candidates for ordination will understand something of that which Saint Paul speaks of in the text. Like him we have arrived at a conclusion. We have made up our minds upon a matter that binds us for life, just as he made up his mind to remain six weeks longer in his Master's service at Ephesus. God help us now and hereafter to say, I have paid Thee my vows, which I promised with my lips and spake with my heart (see Ps. 66:14).

There may be much to plead for our following other lines of life. We do not deny that there are ways of serving God in secular employments and that secular employments may be hallowed by religious motives. But we have chosen our Ephesus. We have put our hands to the plow, and by God's grace we will not look back. We want no Clerical Disabilities' Act to relieve us from what is a voluntary and most welcome service. We have put on the uniform of the captain of our salvation, the sacrificed Savior, and we will wear no other for all the world can give.

But "there are many adversaries." Certainly there are. The man who takes holy orders in the present day does so under very different circumstances from those who did so forty, twenty, or even ten years ago. It is undeniably more difficult to meet a clergyman's responsibilities now than formerly. More is expected in personal exertion and in ministerial efficiency and ability. The air, too, is filled with controversies which may be approached in many ways but which can only be handled in the eye of Eternal Truth in one way. The Romish church has never confronted the English church upon so serious a scale as now in every rank of society.

Nonconformity and infidelity have never before so united their forces against all our efforts to give education to the people. The future is pregnant with possibilities.

Who will attempt to say what will be the outward status of the Church of England twenty or even ten years hence? Who can look forward now, as our forefathers may be assumed to have done, to a settled order of events that shall outlast our time, that shall subsist almost unimpaired when we shall have gone to our account? Out of those days of tranquil and assured repose, we have—it is God's will and providence—passed into this very different period when all around us betrays a foolish impatience of what has been and what is; when change, as change, is spoken of as if it had an inherent (I had almost said, a sacramental) virtue; when blasts of destructive infidel thought sweep through the intellectual atmosphere, paralyzing in numbers of simple souls—even of most devout members—some of the venerable memories and affections of our church; when men are accustomed to look at favorably, to think of patiently, and even, in some cases, to welcome the public abandonment and repudiation of some of the most authoritative and sacred landmarks of our faith.

This is a time, too, when moral and social ideas are not less challenged than higher and eternal truths; when society, if it speak its mind, is profoundly troubled and haunted by a terrible suspicion that it may yet have to reckon with foes more serious than any it has encountered since it rose a thousand years ago out of the chaos of barbarous life. And yet beyond any other class of men who deal, or ought to deal, with the gravest problem of the world of thought—who are or ought to be more directly or intimately interested than any other class of men in the material as well as the spiritual well-being of the people—the clergy must be instinctively alive to these grave questions. As a matter of fact, I can say from experience, they do deter many men who in other days would have taken holy orders from doing so now. Do not let us forget this.

But it is better thus. The strength of the church does not consist in the number of pages of its clerical directory, but in the sum total of moral and spiritual force that she has at command. It is well that we should look upon the difficulties of our time as far as we can as did Saint Paul in his.

They are, I dare to say, as nothing to the man who has an honest heart and a good positive belief. For, after all, my brethren, why is it that we do take orders? Is it not because we believe and are assured that eighteen centuries ago an event, or a series of events, occurred compared with which all that has since occurred, all that can possibly happen, even in our eventful days, must be utterly insignificant? Is it not that, like Saint Paul at Ephesus, we believe and are sure that the everlasting Son of God really entered this world under the ordinary conditions of space and time and died upon the cross for the sins of all men? that He arose from the grave where they had laid Him when He was really dead? that He ascended to the heavenly throne and has been there pleading for us ever since and is doing so at this moment? that God has given us His Spirit and His sacraments?

Is it not because we are convinced that out of the infinite treasury of His love He has done this for us—for each of us—and that the very least we can do is to yield Him our most free and cheerful services under such circumstances, as He may will, in storm or in sunshine, in battle or in repose, in the times of hopefulness or in the days of despondency? To say that it matters little when or where is surely but to say that when seen with a nearer horizon, the tangled web of ecclesiastical and political change dwarfs down to its trite proportions. We shall see nothing before us but Christ crucified and souls perishing all around from lack of knowledge or lack of grace. It must be our duty, as it was the duty of our predecessors—the duty of the great apostle himself—the grand duty of each one of us to bring them within our reach by whatever moral or intellectual instruments we can command, to lead them to the foot of the atoning Cross, to get them a share in the sprinkling of the cleansing blood, to make them know something of that power and wisdom of God that will be to the end of time a stumbling block to the self-righteous and foolishness to the self-opinionated.

For this blessed work, blessed in its usefulness to others, blessed in its reflex effects upon those who undertake it earnestly and in humble dependence upon God's grace, we have now, I dare to say, great opportunities. The difficulties of our time will not stop us; they will rather stimulate and assist us. The evils attending this great work, if we must call them so, are not so formidable, after all. Rome has recently, by her own act, condemned herself to the task of advocating the infallibility of a long list of conflicting and self-contradictory facts and things. Puritanism—to regard our work in all its phases—while it still clutches the pietist formulas of its earlier and better times with convulsive eagerness, is more and more surely forfeiting its own vitality, as it sinks down year by year into that pit of skepticism that its stern refusal of the sacramental uses, graces, and doctrines of the church has already undeniably prepared for it. And so of those other forms of thought that are the implacable enemies of all belief in the name of God and a Divine Christ; they cannot in the long run satisfy a being like man, who has within himself the instinctive presentiment and the ineffaceable evidence of his own immortality. For man the ideas of moral light and coming judgment—ideas that God, revealed in Christ, can alone adequately explain and satisfy—can never be resolved into "a mere sentiment."

The state of things around us now, therefore, is in our favor. We have a better chance of gaining a hearing for our Divine Master than our predecessors of former days, when thought was stagnant and habits and manners fixed; when men frequently were what they were for no other reason but a traditional one; when critics and theorists had not exercised themselves upon the problems that today agitate the human mind, without affording the truth even an opportunity of speaking for itself and then of triumphing. Those who are farthest from the truth have often profound, though yet undeveloped and unrecognized sympathies with it. The King of the intellectual world, Jesus Christ, is ever ruler, even in the midst of His enemies, and the conditions of human life do not alter. Men live and suffer and die just as they did eighteen hundred years ago. The real significance of this short and mysterious passage which we call life is not obliterated by material civilization or by the mental theories of our day.

God grant, my brethren, that, be the scene of your labors what and where it may, you may teach and act—that we may all teach and act—as men who know that they are ministering as dying men to dying men, so that your lives' anxieties and your light afflictions, which are but for a moment—should such in God's providence await you—may work out for you a far more exceeding and eternal weight of glory, through the boundless grace and mercy of Christ Jesus our Lord.

Charge That to My Account

Henry ("Harry") Allan Ironside (1878–1951) was
born in Toronto, Canada, raised in California, and began
preaching when he was converted at the age of fourteen.
He had no formal training for the ministry but devoted
himself to the reading and studying of the Bible. His
early associations were with the Salvation Army, but
then he identified with the Plymouth Brethren and
became one of their most beloved itinerant Bible
teachers. From 1930 to 1948, he pastored the Moody
Church in Chicago. He wrote more than sixty books,
many of which are collections of messages given at
Moody Church and various conferences.

This message is taken from *Charge That to My
Account*, a series of messages given at Moody Church
and published by Loizeaux Brothers in 1931. It is used
by permission of Lillian Ironside Coppin.

Henry ("Harry") Allan Ironside

9

CHARGE THAT TO MY ACCOUNT

> If thou count me therefore a partner, receive him as myself. If he hath wronged thee, or oweth thee ought, put that on mine account; I Paul have written it with mine own hand, I will repay it; albeit I do not say to thee how thou owest unto me even thine own self besides (Philemon 17–19).

SOMEONE HAS SAID THAT this epistle to Philemon is the finest specimen of early private Christian correspondence extant. We should expect this, since it was given by divine inspiration. And yet it all has to do with a thieving runaway slave named Onesimus, who was about to return to his former master.

The history behind the letter, which is deduced from a careful study of the epistle itself, seems to be this: In the city of Colosse dwelt a wealthy Christian man by the name of Philemon, possibly the head of a large household, and like many in that day, he had a number of slaves or bondsmen. Christianity did not immediately overturn the evil custom of slavery, although eventually it was the means of practically driving it out of the whole civilized world. It began by regulating the relation of master and slave, thus bringing untold blessing to those in bondage.

This man Philemon evidently was converted through the ministry of the apostle Paul. Where they met, we are not told; certainly not in the city of Colosse, because in writing the letter to the Colossians, Paul makes it clear that he had never seen the faces of those who formed the Colossian church. You will recall that he labored at Ephesus for a long period. The fame of his preaching and teaching was spread abroad, and we read that "all in Asia heard the word." Among those who thus heard the Gospel message may have been this man Philemon of Colosse, and so he was brought to know Christ.

Some years had gone by, and this slave, Onesimus, had run away. Evidently before going, he had robbed his master. With his ill-gotten gains he had fled to Rome. How he reached there we do not know, but I have no doubt that upon his arrival he had his fling and enjoyed to the full that which had belonged to his master. He did not take God into account, but nevertheless God's eye was upon him when he left his home, and it followed him along the journey from Colosse to Rome. When he reached that great metropolis he was evidently brought into contact with the very man through whom his master, Philemon, had been converted. Possibly Onesimus was arrested because of some further rascality, and in that way came in contact with Paul in prison, or he may have visited him voluntarily. At any rate God, who knows just how to bring the needy sinner and the messenger of the Cross together, saw to it that Onesimus and Paul met face-to-face.

Sam Hadley Finds Jim

Some years ago there happened a wonderful illustration of this very thing: the divine ability to bring the needy sinner and the messenger of Christ together.

When Sam Hadley was in California, just shortly before he died, Dr. J. Wilbur Chapman, that princely man of God, arranged a midnight meeting using the largest theater in the city of Oakland in order to get the message of Hadley before the very people who needed it most. On that night a great procession, maybe one thousand people, from all the different churches, led by the Salvation Army band, wended their way through the main streets of the city. Beginning at 10:30, they marched for one-half hour and then came to the Metropolitan Theater. In a moment or two it was packed from floor to gallery.

I happened to be sitting in the first balcony, looking right down upon the stage. I noticed that every seat on the stage was filled with Christian workers, but when

Sam Hadley stepped forward to deliver the stirring message of the evening, his seat was left vacant. Just as he began to speak, I saw a man who had come in at the rear of the stage slip around from behind the back curtain and stand at one of the wings with his hand up to his ear, listening to the address. Evidently he did not hear very well. In a moment or two he moved to another wing and then on to another one. Finally he came forward to one side of the front part of the stage and stood there listening, but still he could not hear very well. Upon noticing him, Dr. Chapman immediately got up, greeted the poor fellow, brought him to the front, and put him in the very chair that Sam Hadley had occupied. There he listened entranced to the story of Hadley's redemption.

When the speaker had finished, Dr. Chapman arose to close the meeting, and Hadley took Chapman's chair next to this man. Turning to the man he shook hands with him, and they chatted together. When Dr. Chapman was about ready to ask the people to rise and receive the benediction, Hadley suddenly sprang to his feet, and said, "Just a moment, my friends. Before we close, Dr. Chapman, may I say something? When I was on my way from New York to Oakland a couple of weeks ago, I stopped at Detroit. I was traveling in a private car, put at my disposal by a generous Christian manufacturer. While my car was in the yards, I went downtown and addressed a group at a mission. As I finished, an old couple came up and said, 'Mr. Hadley, won't you go home and take supper with us?'

"I replied, 'You must excuse me; I am not at all well, and it is a great strain for me to go out and visit between meetings. I had better go back to the car and rest.'

"They were so disappointed. The mother faltered. 'Oh, Mr. Hadley, we did want to see you so badly about something.'

"'Very well, give me a few moments to lie down and I will go with you.'"

He then told how they sat together in the old-fashioned parlor on the horsehair furniture and talked. They told him their story: "Mr. Hadley, you know we have a son, Jim. Our son was brought up to go to Sunday school and church, and oh, we had such hopes of him. But he had to work out rather early in life and he got into association with worldly men and went down and down and down. By and by he came under the power of strong drink. We shall never forget the first time he came home drunk. Sometimes he would never get home at all until the early hours of the morning. Our hearts were breaking over him. One time he did not come all night, but early in the morning, after we had waited through a sleepless night for him, he came in hurriedly, with a pale face and said, 'Folks, I cannot stay; I must get out. I did something when I was drunk last night, and if it is found out, it will go hard with me. I am not going to stay here and blot your name.' He kissed us both and left, and until recently we have never seen nor heard of him.

"Mr. Hadley, here is a letter that just came from a friend who lives in California, and he tells us, 'I am quite certain that I saw your son, Jim, in San Francisco. I was coming down on a street car and saw him waiting for a car. I was carried by a block. I hurried back, but he had boarded another car and was gone. I know it was Jim.'

"He is still living, Mr. Hadley, and we are praying that God will save him yet. You are going to California to have meetings out there. Daily we will be kneeling here praying that God will send our boy, Jim, to hear you, and perhaps when he learns how God saved one poor drunkard, he will know there is hope also for him. Will you join us in daily prayer?"

"I said I would, and we prayed together. They made me promise that every day at a given hour, Detroit time, I would lift my heart to God in fellowship with them, knowing that they were kneeling in that room, praying to God that He would reach Jim and give me the opportunity of bringing him to Christ. That was two weeks ago. I have kept my promise every day. My friends, this is my first meeting in California, and here is Jim. Tonight he was drinking in a saloon on Broadway as the great procession passed. He heard the singing, followed us to the theater, and said, 'I believe I will go in.' He hurried up here, but it was too late. Every place was filled, and the police officer said, 'We cannot allow another person to go inside.' Jim thought, 'This is just my luck. Even if I want to go and hear the Gospel, I cannot. I will go back to the saloon.' He started back; then he returned determined to see if there was not some way to get in. He came in the back door and finally sat in my own chair. Friends, Jim wants Christ, and I ask you all to pray for him."

There that night we saw that poor fellow drop on his knees and confess his sin and guilt and accept Christ as his Savior. The last sight we had of Jim was when J. Wilbur Chapman and he were on their way to the Western Union Telegraph office to send the joyful message: "God heard your prayers. My soul is saved." Oh, what a God, lover of sinners that He is! How He delights to reach the lost and needy!

"He Delighteth in Mercy"

This same God was watching over Onesimus. He saw him when he stole that money and as he fled from his master's house. He watched him on his way to Rome and in due time brought him face-to-face with Paul. Through that same precious Gospel that had been blessed to the salvation of Philemon, Onesimus, the thieving runaway slave, was also saved, and another star was added to the Redeemer's crown.

Then I can imagine Onesimus coming to Paul and saying, "Now, Paul, I want your advice. There is a matter that is troubling me. You know my master, Philemon. I must confess that I robbed him and ran away. I feel now that I must go back and try to make things right."

One evidence that people are really born of God is their effort to make restitution for wrong done in the past. They want a good conscience both before God and man.

"Paul, ought I to go back in accordance with the Roman law? I have nothing to pay, and I don't know just what to do. I do not belong to myself, and it is quite impossible to ever earn anything to make up for the loss. Will you advise me what to do?"

Paul might have said, "I know Philemon well. He has a tender, kind, loving heart and a forgiving spirit. I will write him a note and ask him to forgive you, and that will make everything all right."

But he did not do that. Why? I think that he wanted to give us a wonderful picture of the great gospel of vicarious substitution. One of the primary aspects of the work of the Cross is substitution. The Lord Jesus Christ Himself paid the debt that we owe to the infinite God in order that when forgiveness came to us it would be on a perfectly righteous basis. Paul, who had himself been justified through the Cross, now says, "I will write a letter to Philemon and undertake to become your surety. You go back to Philemon and present my letter. You do not need to plead your own case; just give him my letter."

We see Onesimus with that message from Paul safely hidden in his wallet, hurrying back to Colosse. Imagine Philemon standing on the portico of his beautiful residence, looking down the road and suddenly exclaiming, "Why, who is that? It certainly looks like that scoundrel, Onesimus! But surely he would not have the face to come back. Still, it looks very much like him. I will just watch and wait."

A little later, he says, "I declare, it *is* Onesimus! He seems to be coming to the house. I suppose he has had a hard time in the world. The stolen money is all gone, and now perhaps he is coming to beg for pardon."

As he comes up the pathway, Onesimus calls, "Master, Master!"

"Well, Onesimus, are you home again?"

"Yes, Master, read this, please."

No other word would Onesimus speak for himself; Paul's letter would explain all.

Philemon takes the letter, opens it, and begins to read: *Paul, a prisoner of Jesus Christ* (v. 1).

"Why Onesimus, where did you meet Paul? Did you see him personally?"

"Yes, Master, in the prison in Rome; he led me to Christ."

Unto Philemon our dearly beloved, and fellowlaborer (v. 1).

"Little enough I have ever done, but that is just like Paul."

And to our beloved Apphia (v. 2). (That was Mrs. Philemon.)

"Come here, Apphia. Here is a letter from Paul." When Mrs. Philemon sees Onesimus, she exclaims, "Are you back?"

One can imagine her mingled disgust and indignation as she sees him standing there. But Philemon says: "Yes, my dear, not a word. Here is a letter for us to read—a letter from Paul."

Running on down the letter he comes to this: *Yet for love's sake I rather beseech thee, being such an one as Paul the aged, and now also a prisoner of Jesus Christ. I beseech thee for my son Onesimus* (vv. 9–10).

"Think of that! He must have been putting it over on Paul in some way or another."

Whom I have begotten in my bonds (v. 10). "I wonder if he told him anything about the money he stole from us. I suppose he has been playing the religious game with Paul."

Which in time past was to thee unprofitable (v. 11).

"I should say he was."

But now profitable to thee and to me (v. 12).

"I am not so sure of that."

Whom I have sent again (v. 12).

"Paul must have thought a lot of him. If he didn't serve him any better than he did me, he would not get much out of him." He goes on reading through the letter.

"Well, well, that rascally, thieving liar! Maybe Paul believes that he is saved, but I will never believe it unless I find out that he owned up to the wrong he did me."

What is this? *If he hath wronged thee, or oweth thee ought, put that on mine account; I Paul have written it with mine own hand, I will repay it: albeit I do not say to thee how thou owest unto me even thine own self besides* (v. 18–19).

Oh, I think in a moment Philemon was conquered. "Why," he says, "it is all out then. He has confessed his sin. He has acknowledged his thieving, owned his guilt, and, just think, Paul, that dear servant of God, suffering in prison for Christ's sake, says: *Put that on my account. I will settle everything for him.* Paul becomes his surety." It was just as though Paul should write today: "Charge that to my account!"

A Gospel Picture

Is not this a picture of the Gospel? A picture of what the Savior has done for every repentant soul? I think I see Him as he brings the needy, penitent sinner into the presence of God and says, "My Father, he has wronged Thee, he owes Thee much, but all has been charged to My account. Let him go free." How could the Father turn aside the prayer of His Son after that death of shame and sorrow on Calvary's cross, when He took our blame upon Himself and suffered in our stead?

But now observe it is not only that Paul offered to become Onesimus's surety, it was not merely that he offered to settle everything for Onesimus in regard to the past, but he provided for his future too. He says to Philemon: *If thou count me therefore a partner, receive him as myself* (v. 17).

Is not that another aspect of our salvation? We are "accepted in the beloved" (Eph. 1:6). The blessed Savior brings the redeemed one into the presence of the Father and says, "My Father, if thou countest Me the partner of Thy throne, receive him as Myself." Paul says, *Not now as a servant, but above a servant, a brother beloved, specially to me, but how much more unto thee, both in the flesh, and in the Lord?* (Philem. 16). He is to take the place, not of a bondsman, but of an honored member of the family and a brother in Christ. Think of it—once a poor, thieving, runaway slave and now a recognized servant of Christ, made welcome for Paul's sake. Thus our Father saves the lawless, guilty sinner and makes him welcome for Jesus' sake, treating him as He treats His own beloved Son.

> Jesus paid it all,
> All to Him I owe;
> Sin had left a crimson stain
> He washed it white as snow.

And now every redeemed one is in Christ before God—yea, "made the righteousness of God in him" (2 Cor. 5:21). Oh, wondrous love! Justice is satisfied. What a picture we have here then of substitution and acceptance. The apostle Paul gave the epitome of it all for us: "[Jesus our Lord] was delivered for our offences, and was raised again for our justification" (Rom. 4:25).

We are accepted in the Beloved. The Lord Jesus became our Surety, settled for all our past, and has provided for all our future. In the book of Proverbs (11:15), there is a very striking statement, "He that is surety for a stranger shall smart for it: and he that hateth suretiship is sure." These words were written centuries before the Cross, to warn men of what is still a very common ground for failure and ruin in business life. To go surety for a stranger is a very dangerous thing, as thousands have learned to their sorrow. It is poor policy to take such a risk unless you are prepared to lose.

But there was One who knew to the full what all the consequences of His act would be and yet, in grace, deigned to become "surety for a stranger." Meditate upon these wonderful words: "For ye know the grace of our Lord Jesus Christ, that, though he was rich, yet for your sakes he became poor, that ye through his poverty might be rich" (2 Cor. 8:9). He was the stranger's Surety.

A surety is one who stands good for another. Many a

man will do this for a friend long known and trusted, but no wise man will so act for a stranger, unless he is prepared to lose. But it was when we were strangers and foreigners and enemies and alienated in our minds by wicked works that Jesus in grace became our Surety. "Christ also hath once suffered for sins, the just for the unjust, that he might bring us to God" (1 Peter 3:18).

All we owed was exacted from Him when He suffered upon the tree for sins not His own. He could then say, "I restored that which I took not away" (Ps. 69:4). Bishop Lowth's beautiful rendering of Isaiah 53:7 reads: "It was exacted and He became answerable." This is the very essence of the Gospel message. He died in my place; He paid my debt.

How fully He proved the truth of the words quoted from Proverbs when He suffered on that cross of shame! How He had to smart for it when God's awful judgment against sin fell upon Him. But He wavered not! In love to God and to the strangers whose Surety He had become, "He endured the cross, despising the shame" (Heb. 12:2).

His sorrows are now forever past. He has paid the debt, met every claim in perfect righteousness. The believing sinner is cleared of every charge, and God is fully glorified.

> He bore on the tree
> The sentence for me,
> And now both the Surety
> And sinner are free.

None other could have met the claims of God's holiness against the sinner and have come out triumphant at last. He alone could atone for sin. Because He has settled every claim, God has raised Him from the dead and seated Him at His own right hand in highest glory.

Have you trusted the stranger's Surety? If not, turn to Him now while grace is free.

NOTES

A Prisoner's Dying Thoughts

Alexander Maclaren (1826–1910) was one of Great
Britain's most famous preachers. While pastoring the
Union Chapel, Manchester (1858–1903), he became
known as "the prince of expository preachers." Rarely
active in denominational or civic affairs, Maclaren
invested his time in studying the Word in the original
and sharing its truths with others in sermons that are
still models of effective expository preaching. He
published a number of books of sermons and climaxed
his ministry by publishing his monumental *Expositions
of Holy Scripture*.

   This message is taken from *The Secret of Power*
published by Funk and Wagnalls Company in 1902.

Alexander Maclaren

10

A PRISONER'S DYING THOUGHTS

I am now ready to be offered, and the time of my departure is at hand. I have fought a good fight, I have finished my course, I have kept the faith: henceforth there is laid up for me a crown of righteousness (2 Timothy 4:6–8).

PAUL'S LONG DAY'S WORK is nearly done. He is a prisoner in Rome, all but forsaken by his friends, in hourly expectation of another summons before Nero. To appear before him was, he says, like putting his head into the mouth of the lion (see 2 Tim. 4:17). His horizon was darkened by sad anticipations of decaying faith and growing corruptions in the church. What a road he had traveled since that day when, on the way to Damascus, he saw the living Christ and heard the words of His mouth!

It had been but a failure of a life, if judged by ordinary standards. He had suffered the loss of all things, had thrown away position and prospects, had exposed himself to sorrows and toils, had been all his days a poor man and solitary, had been hunted, despised, laughed at by Jew and Gentile, worried and badgered even by so-called brethren, loved the less the more he loved. And now the end is near. A prison and the headsman's sword are the world's wages to its best teacher. When Nero is on the throne, the only possible place for Paul is the dungeon opening on to the scaffold. Better to be the martyr than the Caesar.

These familiar words of our text bring before us a very sweet and wonderful picture of the prisoner so near his end. How beautifully they show his calm waiting for the last hour and the bright forms that lightened for him the darkness of his cell! Many since have gone to their rest with their hearts stayed on the same thoughts, though their lips could not speak them to our listening ears. Let us be thankful for them and pray that for ourselves, when we come to that hour, the same quiet heroism and the same sober hope mounting to calm certainty may be ours.

These words refer to the present: "The time of my departure is at hand"; the past: "I have kept the faith"; and the future: "Henceforth there is laid up . . . a crown."

The Present

We notice first the quiet courage which looks death full in the face without a tremor. The language implies that Paul knows his death hour is all but here. As the Revised Version more accurately gives it, "I am already being offered"—the process is begun, his sufferings at the moment are, as it were, the initial steps of his sacrifice—"and the time of my departure is come." The tone in which he tells Timothy this is very noticeable. There is no sign of excitement, no tremor of emotion, no affectation of stoicism in the simple sentences. He is not playing up to a part, nor pretending to be anything that he is not. If ever language sounded perfectly simple and genuine, this does.

And the occasion of the whole section is as remarkable as the tone. He is led to speak about himself at all only in order to enforce his exhortation to Timothy to put his shoulder to the wheel and do his work for Christ with all his might. All he wishes to say is simply, Do your work with all your might, for I am going off the field. But having begun on that line of thought, he is carried on to say more than was needed for his immediate purpose and thus inartificially to let us see what was filling his mind.

And the subject into which he subsides after these lofty thoughts is as remarkable as either tone or occasion. Minute directions about such small matters as books and parchments and perhaps a warm cloak for winter and homely details about the movements of the little group of his friends immediately follow. All this shows with what a perfectly unforced courage Paul fronted his fate and looked death in the eyes. The anticipation did not dull his interest in God's work in the world, as witness the warnings and exhortations of the context. It did not withdraw his sympathies from his companions. It did not hinder him from pursuing his studies and pursuits, nor from providing for small matters of daily convenience. If ever a man was free from any taint of fanaticism or morbid enthusiasm, it was this man waiting so calmly in his prison for his death.

There is great beauty and force in the expressions that he uses for death here. He will not soil his lips with its ugly name, but calls it an offering and a departure. There is a widespread unwillingness to say the word *death*. It falls on men's hearts like clods on a coffin—so all people and languages have adopted euphemisms for it, fair names that wrap silk around its dart and somewhat hide its face. But there are two opposite reasons for their use—terror and confidence. Some men dare not speak of death because they dread it so much and try to put some kind of shield between themselves and the very thought of it by calling it something less dreadful to them than itself. Some men, on the other hand, are familiar with the thought, and though it is solemn, it is not altogether repellent to them. Gazing on death with the thoughts and feelings that Jesus Christ has given them concerning it, they see it in new aspects which take away much of its blackness. And so they do not feel inclined to use the ugly old name, but had rather call it by some which reflect the gentler aspect that it now wears to them. So *sleep*, and *rest* and the like are the names which have almost driven the other out of the New Testament—witness of the fact that in inmost reality Jesus Christ has "abolished death" (2 Tim. 1:10), however the physical portion of it may still remain master of our bodies.

But looking for a moment at the specific metaphors used here, we have first, that of an *offering*, or more particularly of a drink offering, or *libation*, "I am already being poured out." No doubt the special reason for the selection of this figure here is Paul's anticipation of a violent death. The shedding of his blood was to be an offering poured out like some costly wine upon the altar, but the power of the figure reaches far beyond that special application of it. We may all make our deaths a sacrifice, an offering to God, for we may yield up our will to God's will and so turn that last struggle into an act of worship and self-surrender. When we recognize His hand, when we submit our wills to His purposes, when we live unto the Lord, if we live, and die unto Him, if we die, then death will lose all its terror and most of its pain and will become for us what it was to Paul, a true offering up of self in thankful worship. We may even say that so we shall in a certain subordinate sense be "made conformable unto his death" who committed His spirit into His Father's hands and laid down His life of His own will. The essential character and far-reaching effects of this sacrifice we cannot imitate, but we can so yield up our wills to God and leave life so willingly and trustfully as that death shall make our sacrifice complete.

Another more familiar and equally striking figure is next used when Paul speaks of the time of his "departure." The thought is found in most tongues. Death is a going away, or, as Peter calls it (with a glance, possibly, at the special meaning of the word in the Old Testament, as well as its use in the solemn statement of the theme of converse on the Mountain of Transfiguration), an exodus. But the well-worn image receives new depth and sharpness of outline in Christianity. To those who have learned the meaning of Christ's resurrection and who feed their souls on the hopes that it warrants, death is merely a change of place or state, an accident affecting locality and little more. We have had plenty of changes before. Life has been one long series of departures. This is different from the others mainly in that it is the last and that to go away from this visible and fleeting show, where we wander aliens among things that have no true kindred with us, is to go home, where there will be no more pulling up the tent pegs and toiling across the deserts in monotonous change. How strong is the conviction, spoken in that name for death, that the essential life lasts on quite unaltered through it all! How slight the else formidable thing is made. We may change climates and for the stormy bleakness of life may have the long still days of heaven, but we do not change ourselves. We lose nothing worth keeping when we leave behind the body, as a dress not fitted for home, where we are going. We but travel one more stage, though it be the last, and part of it be in pitchy darkness. Some pass over it as in a fiery chariot, like Paul and many a martyr. Some have to toil through it with slow steps and bleeding feet and fainting hearts, but all may have a Brother with them and holding His hand may find that the journey is not so hard as they feared and the home from which they shall remove no more better than they hoped when they hoped the most.

The Past

We have here, too, the peaceful look backward. There is something very noteworthy in the threefold aspect under which his past life presents itself to the apostle, who is so soon to leave it. He thinks of it as a contest, as a race, as a stewardship.

A race suggests the tension of a long struggle with opposing wrestlers who have tried to throw him, but in vain. The world, both of men and things, has had to be grappled with and mastered. His own sinful nature and especially his animal nature has had to be kept under by sheer force, and every moment has been resistance to subtle omnipresent forces that have sought to thwart his aspirations and hamper his performances. His successes have had to be fought for, and everything that he has done has been done after a struggle. So is it with all noble life; so will it be to the end.

He thinks of life as *a race*. That speaks of continuous advance in one direction and, more emphatically still, of effort that sets the lungs panting and strains every muscle to the utmost.

He thinks of it as a *stewardship*. He has kept the faith (whether by that word we are to understand the body of truth believed or the act of believing) as a sacred deposit committed to him, of which he has been a good steward, and which he is now ready to return to his Lord. There is much in these letters to Timothy about keeping treasures entrusted to one's care. Timothy is bid to keep "that good thing which was committed unto thee" (2 Tim. 1:14), as Paul here declares that he has done. Nor is such guarding of a precious deposit confined to us stewards on earth, but the apostle is sure that his loving Lord, to whom he has entrusted himself, will with like tenderness and carefulness "keep that which [he has] committed unto him against that day" (2 Tim. 1:12). The confidence in that faithful Keeper made it possible for Paul to be faithful to his trust, and as a steward who was bound by all ties to his Lord, to guard His possessions and administer His affairs. Life was full of voices urging him to give up the faith. Bribes and threats, and his own sense-bound nature, and the constant whispers of the world had tempted him all along the road to fling it away as a worthless thing, but he had kept it safe. Now, nearing the end of the account, he can put his hand on the secret place near his heart where it lies and feel that it is there, ready to be restored to his Lord with the thankful confession, "Thy pound hath gained ten pounds" (Luke 19:16).

So life looks to this man in his retrospect as mainly a field for struggle, effort, and fidelity. This world is not to be for us an enchanted garden of delights, any more than it should appear a dreary desert of disappointment and woe. But it should be to us mainly a palaestra, or gymnasium and exercising ground. You cannot expect many flowers or much grass in the place where men wrestle and run. We need not mind much though it be bare, if we can only stand firm on the hard earth, nor lament that there are so few delights to stay our eyes from the goal. We are here for serious work; let us not be too eager for pleasures that may hinder our efforts and weaken our vigor, but be content to lap up a hasty draught from the brooks by the way, and then on again to the fight.

Such a view of life makes it radiant and fair while it lasts, and makes the heart calm when the hour comes to leave it all behind. So thinking of the past, there may be a sense of not unwelcome lightening from a load of responsibility when we have gotten all the stress and strain of the conflict behind us, and have at any rate not been altogether beaten. We may feel like a captain who has brought his ship safe across the Atlantic through foul weather and past many an iceberg, and gives a great sigh of relief as he hands over the charge to the pilot, who will take her across the harbor bar and bring her to her anchorage in the landlocked bay where no tempests rave any more forever.

Prosaic theologians have sometimes wondered at the estimate which Paul here makes of his past services and faithfulness, but the wonder is surely unnecessary. It is very striking to notice the difference between his judgment of himself while he was still in the thick of the conflict, and now when he is nearing the end. Then, one main hope which animated all his toils and nerved him for the sacrifice of life itself was "that I might finish my course with joy" (Acts 20:24). Now, in the quiet of his dungeon, that hope is fulfilled, and triumphant thoughts, like shining angels, keep him company in his solitude. Then he struggles, and wrestles, touched by the haunting fear lest after that he has preached to others he himself should be rejected. Now the dread has passed, and a meek hope stands by his side.

What is this change of feeling but an instance of what, thank God, we so often see, that at the end the heart which has been bowed with fears and self-depreciation is filled with peace? They who tremble most during the conflict are most likely to look back with solid satisfaction, while they who never knew a fear all along the course will often have them surging in upon their souls too late and will see the past in a new lurid light when they are powerless to change it. Blessed is the man who thus fears always. At the end he will have hope. The past struggles are joyful in memory, as the mountain ranges, which were all black rock and white snow while we toiled up their inhospitable steeps, lie purple in the mellowing distance, and burn like fire as the sunset strikes their peaks. Many a wild winter's day has a fair cloudless close and lingering opal hues diffused through all the quiet sky. "At evening time it shall be light" (Zech. 14:7). Though we go all our lives mourning and timid, there may yet be granted us before the end some vision of the true significance of these lives and some humble hope that they have not been wholly in vain.

Such an estimate has nothing in common with self-complacency. It coexists with a profound consciousness of many a sin, many a defeat, and much unfaithfulness. It belongs only to a man who, conscious of these, is "looking for the mercy of our Lord Jesus Christ unto eternal life" (Jude 21), and is the direct result, not the antagonist, of lowly self-abasement and contrite faith in Him, by whom alone our stained selves and poor broken services can ever be acceptable. Let us learn too that the only life that bears being looked back upon is a life of Christian devotion and effort. It shows fairer when seen in the strange cross lights that come when we stand on the boundary of two worlds with the white radiance of eternity beginning to master the vulgar oil lamps of earth than when seen by these alone. All others have their shabbiness and their selfishness disclosed then. I remember once seeing a mob of revelers streaming out from a masked ball in a London theater in the early morning sunlight; draggled and heavy-eyed, the rouge showing on the cheeks and the shabby tawdriness of the foolish costumes pitilessly revealed by the pure light. So will many a life look when the day dawns and the wild riot ends in its unwelcome beams.

The one question for us all then will be, Have I lived for Christ and by Him? Let it be the one question for us now, and let it be answered, Yes. Then we shall have at the last a calm confidence, equally far removed from presumption and from dread, which will let us look back on life, though it be full of failures and sins, with peace, and forward with humble hope of the reward which we shall receive from His mercy.

The Future

The climax of all is the triumphant look forward. "Henceforth there is laid up for me a crown of righteousness." In harmony with the images of the conflict and the race, the crown here is not the emblem of sovereignty, but of victory, as indeed is almost without exception the case in the New Testament. The idea of the royal dignity of Christians in the future is set forth rather under the emblem of association with Christ on His throne, while the wreath on their brows is the coronal of laurel, "meed of mighty conquerors," or the twine of leaves given to him who, panting, touched the goal. The reward then that is meant by the emblem, whatever be its essence, comes through effort and conflict. A man is not crowned, except he strive (see 2 Tim. 2:5).

That crown, according to other words of Scripture, consists of *life* or *glory*—that is to say, the issue and outcome of believing service and faithful stewardship here is the possession of the true life, which stands in union with God, in measure so great and in quality so wondrous that it lies on the pure locks of the victors like a flashing diadem, all ablaze with light in a hundred jewels. The completion and exaltation of our nature and characters by the receiving of "life" so sovereign and transcendent that it is "glory" is the consequence of all Christian effort here in the lower levels, where the natural life is always weakness and sometimes shame, and the spiritual life is at the best but a hidden glory and a struggling spark. There is no profit in seeking to gaze into that light of glory so as to discern the shapes of those who walk in it or the elements of its lambent flames. Enough that in its gracious beauty transfigured souls move as in their native atmosphere. Enough that even our dim vision can see that they have for their companion "One like unto the Son of man" (Rev. 1:13). It is Christ's own life that they share; it is Christ's own glory that irradiates them.

That crown is "a crown of righteousness" (James 1:12) in another sense from that in which it is "a crown of life" (Rev. 2:10). The latter expression indicates the material, if we may say so, of which it is woven, but the former rather points to the character to which it belongs or is given. Righteousness alone can receive that reward. It is not the struggle or the conflict that wins it, but the character evolved in the struggle; not the works of strenuous service, but the moral nature expressed in these. There is such congruity between righteousness and the crown of life that it can be laid on none other head but that of a righteous man, and if it could, all its amaranthine flowers would shrivel and fall when they touched an impure brow. It is, then, the crown of righteousness, as belonging by its very nature to such characters alone.

But whatever is the essential congruity between the character and the crown, we have to remember too that, according to this apostle's constant teaching, the righteousness which clothes us in fair raiment and has a natural right to the wreath of victory is a gift, as truly as the crown itself, and is given to us all on condition of our simple trust in Jesus Christ. If we are to be found of Him in peace, without spot and blameless (see 2 Peter 3:14), we must be found in Him, not having our own righteousness, but that which is ours through faith in Christ (see Phil. 3:9). Toil and conflict and anxious desire to be true to our responsibilities will do much for a man, but they will not bring him that righteousness which brings down on the head the crown of life. We must trust to Christ to give us the righteousness in which we are justified and to give us the righteousness by the working out of which in our lives and characters we are fitted for that great reward. He crowns our works and selves with exuberant and unmerited honors, but what He crowns is His own gift to us, and His great love must bestow both the righteousness and the crown.

The crown is given at a time called by Paul "at that day," which is not the near day of his martyrdom, but that of His Lord's appearing. He does not speak of the fullness of the reward as being ready for him at death, but as being henceforth laid up for him in heaven. So he looks forward beyond the grave. The immediate future after death was to his view a period of blessedness indeed but not yet full. The state of the dead in Christ was a state of consciousness, a state of rest, a state of felicity, but also a state of expectation. To the full height of their present capacity they who sleep in Jesus are blessed, being still in His embrace and their spirits pillowed on His heart, nor so sleeping that, like drowsy infants, they know not where they lie so safe, but only sleeping in so much as they rest from weariness and have closed their eyes to the ceaseless turmoil of this fleeting world and are lapped about forever with the sweet, unbroken consciousness that they are "present with the Lord." What perfect repose, perfect fruition of all desires, perfect union with the perfect End and Object of all their beings, perfect exemption from all sorrow, tumult, and sin can bring of blessedness, that they possess in overmeasure unfailingly. And, in addition, they still know the joy of hope and have carried that jewel with them into another world, for they wait for the redemption of the body, in the reception of which, "at that day," their lives will be filled up to a yet fuller measure and gleam with a more lustrous glory. Now they rest and wait. Then shall they be crowned.

Nor must self-absorbed thoughts be allowed to bound our anticipations of that future. It is no solitary blessedness to which Paul looked forward. Alone in his dungeon, alone before his judge when no man stood with him, soon to be alone in his martyrdom, he leaps up in spirit at the thought of the mighty crowd among whom he will stand in that day, on every head a crown, in every heart the same love to the Lord whose life is in them all and makes them all one. So we may cherish the hope of a social heaven. Man's course begins in a garden, but it ends in a city. The final condition will be the perfection of human society. There all who love Christ will be drawn together and old ties, broken for a little while here, be reknit in yet holier form, never to be parted more.

Ah, friends, the all-important question for each of us is how may we have such a hope, like a great sunset light shining into the western windows of our souls? There is but one answer—trust Christ. That is enough. Nothing else is. Is your life built on Jesus Christ? Are you trusting your salvation to Him? Are you giving Him your love and service? Does your life bear looking at today? Will it bear looking at in death? Will it bear His looking at in judgment?

If you can humbly say, To me to live is Christ, then is it well. Living by Him we may fight and conquer, may win and obtain. Living by Him, we may be ready quietly to lie down when the time comes and may have all the future filled with the blaze of a great hope that glows brighter as the darkness thickens. That peaceful hope will not leave us until consciousness fails, and then when it has ceased to guide us Christ Himself will lead us, scarcely knowing where we are, through the waters, and when we open our half-bewildered eyes in brief wonder, the first thing we see will be His welcoming smile, and His voice will say, as a tender surgeon might to a little child waking after an operation, "It is over." We lift our hands wondering and find wreaths on our poor brows. We lift our eyes and lo! all about us a crowned crowd of conquerors,

> And with the morn those angel faces smile
> Which we have loved long since, and lost awhile.

NOTES

The Threefold Secret of a Great Life

George W. Truett (1867–1944) was perhaps the best-known Southern Baptist preacher of his day. He pastored the First Baptist Church of Dallas, Texas, from 1897 until his death and saw it grow both in size and influence. Active in denominational ministry, Truett served as president of the Southern Baptist Convention and for five years was president of the Baptist World Alliance, but he was known primarily as a gifted preacher and evangelist. Nearly a dozen books of his sermons were published.

This sermon is taken from *A Quest for Souls,* published in 1945 by Harper and Brothers, New York.

George W. Truett

11

THE THREEFOLD SECRET OF A GREAT LIFE

Brethren, I count not myself to have apprehended: but this one thing I do, forgetting those things which are behind, and reaching forth unto those things which are before, I press toward the mark for the prize of the high calling of God in Christ Jesus (Philippians 3:13–14).

SOMEBODY HAS WELL SAID that "the proper study of mankind is man" (Alexander Pope). The study of biography, therefore, is always a most fascinating and helpful study. Everybody who is normal is interested keenly in the lives of people who have succeeded. We would know all that we may about them, about their beginnings, their struggles, their habits, about their viewpoints in life. This morning I would direct your attention for a little while to the most remarkable Christian of the centuries, namely, the apostle Paul. He was, and is, the greatest single credential that Christ's Gospel has ever produced. One day in writing to his favorite church, the Philippian church, in a burst of confidence it would seem, he lets us into the secret of his marvelous life. We are to study that threefold secret for a little while this morning. Mark his words: "This one thing I do, forgetting those things which are behind, and reaching forth unto those things which are before, I press toward the mark for the prize of the high calling of God in Christ Jesus."

Wholehearted Concentration

In those words, this greatest of all Christians states the threefold secret of his incomparable life. We will do well to look at that threefold secret today. The first element in it is the element of wholehearted concentration. "This one thing I do"—not a dozen things, not

127

even two things, but "this one thing I do." No life can be very great or very happy or very useful without this element of concentration. Everyone should have a work to do and know what it is and do it with all his might. Decision is energy, and energy is power, and power is confidence, and confidence to a remarkable degree contributes to success. Many a man in life has failed not from lack of ability, but from lack of this element of concentration. The whole world is witness to its power. Turn to any realm that you will, and the vital meaning of concentration stands out in all human life after the most striking fashion.

Take *the business world*, and the element of concentration there is of prime importance if success is to be achieved. The very watchwords in the business world magnify this element of concentration. They talk to us about *specialization* and *consolidation* and *incorporation*, on and on, giving emphasis in all such words to the meaningful quality of concentration. A short time ago one of the world's most successful businessmen was waited upon by a group of young men who sought his counsel about how to succeed, and he gave them this laconic advice: "Young gentlemen, get all your eggs into one basket, and then watch that basket." It was his way of giving emphasis to the tremendous value of concentration. The day for the jack-of-all-trades has passed. A man must do one thing and do it with all his might. The professional man understands that. The lawyer who is minded to reach the topmost rung of his high calling sets himself with all diligence and devotedness to that calling and does not dissipate his energies on a half dozen other callings, as in the other days men sometimes did. The physician understands that. The day of the specialist has come. The teacher understands that. In all the world about us men understand that this winning element, stated by Paul as the first element, humanly speaking, of his marvelous career, is indispensable to success, namely, the power of concentration—"this one thing I do."

And when we turn to *the world of science* and look at

the notable scientists, that truth of concentration seems to be written in their lives as with letters of living fire. Edison with all devotedness concentrated his energies in the realm of electricity and was constantly surprising the world by his marvelous discoveries. And the Wright brothers, with all their devotedness, gave themselves to the mastery of the secrets of the air and constantly surprised us by their revelations.

When we come to the highest realm of all—*the realm religious*—this element of concentration there holds sway just as in these other realms. No man can serve two masters. One must be our Master, and Jesus stands above all mankind and says: If you would be my disciple, then I tell you I must come first. I must come before father or mother or the dearest loved one of your life. I must come before your own business or your own property. I must come before your own life. I must be Lord of all, or I will not be Lord at all.

Now, you would not trust your soul's eternal welfare to a proffered Savior who would ask or allow anything less than that He should be first. "Ye shall seek me, and find me, when ye search for me with all your heart" (Jer. 29:13). I care not what may be a man's difficulties or doubts in the world religious, if only such man, with definiteness of purpose, with wholeheartedness of aim, shall set himself to seek God's light and leading, I know that he will find Him. "In the day that thou seekest me with thy whole heart, I will be found of thee" (my paraphrase). Many a Christian man follows Christ afar off and limps and grovels in the Christian life because he is seeking to adjust himself in life to giving Christ some secondary place, and Christ will not have it. Concentration is a prime requisite in the victorious life anywhere.

Wise Forgetfulness of the Past

In the second place the great Christian leads us to the consideration of a second secret explanatory of his marvelous career and that is that he cultivated a wise forgetfulness of the past. It rings like a trumpet blast in this Bible that we are to remember certain things that we ought to remember. That word *remember* rings out like a bugle blast again and again in the Bible. But along with the factor of wisely remembering there is to go that other important factor of wisely forgetting. Many a man goes hobbled and crippled through life and never does come to the highest and best because he cannot forget certain things that ought to be forgotten by him.

And what are some of the things that we ought every one to forget? Let me run over a brief list. *We ought every one to learn how practically to forget our blunders.* What blunderers we all are, and how many blunders we all make! Every man must learn how to forget his own blunders, or he will go manacled and crippled to his grave. The old saying comes in point right clearly, that the best of men are but men at the best. We are to learn, therefore, how to forget our blunders. Ebenezer was a field of defeat before it rang with the songs of victory. We are to learn how to take our very blunders and make them bridges over which we shall span the chasms and go to better days.

And what else are we to learn how to forget? *We are to learn how to forget our losses.* In human life losses of all kinds come more or less in our experiences. We are to learn how to get past them and practically to forget them. I have observed no more painfully tragical sight than a strong, alert man down in spirit, singing his dirges, and chanting his jeremiads because he had lost some property. I am thinking now of a man whose property burned up a day or two after the insurance had expired, and all was a total loss. There he was without property at all, in the gray of that early morning, and with his face in his hands he kept chanting the pitiful cry: "I have lost all!" Presently his tiny little girl of four or five summers came to him all puzzled and said: "Why, no, Papa, you have not lost all. You have me and Mamma left!" And it took that to summon him and to hearten him and to bring him back to sobriety and to right thinking. No man is to whine and mope and go down because losses come here and there and yonder. But he is to learn how to get past them and to forget them.

What else are we to forget? *We are to learn how to forget life's injuries.* It would seem that in this world of ours with its rivalries and competitions and frictions and alienations, it is difficult to get past the injuries that come in human life. And yet I tell you, my brother men, if for any cause you are cherishing hate in your hearts, then you have lost the highest perspective of life and cannot have the highest perspective of life as long as the poison of hate is allowed in your hearts and in your lives. A man is terribly hindered and has around him a ball and a chain if in his heart he cherishes something that says: "I will lie awake at nights, and I will turn many a corner, and I will await my day to get even with some man for some cruel dart that he throws at me." Big men do not hate. Big men do not cherish resentments. Big men put them down and out and go their way and refuse to harbor them. They refuse to let them rankle like poisons in the heart thus to vitiate every high thing that the spirit should hold most dear.

What else are we to forget? *We are to learn how to forget our successes.* More men have been spoiled by success than you and I can begin to measure. There is danger in success, anywhere, for any man. If a man can bear success, he can bear anything. Easier far can the human spirit bear adversity than it can bear prosperity. It is better any day to go to the house of mourning than to the house of feasting, for in the house of feasting the human spirit is lifted up, and pride always goes before destruction, and a haughty spirit always goes before a fall. When Uzziah of old came to his day of remarkable prosperity, then it was that the Bible tells us his heart was lifted up to destruction. The history of the rich American family stands out like a mountain range, that every third generation of such family goes to defeat and failure and poverty. The first generation wins success, the second generation spends it, and the third generation goes the downward way to poverty and failure. We are to learn how to forget our successes. If a man does not learn what success is for—any kind of success, financial success, political success, social success, intellectual success, any kind of success—if he does not learn what it is for, the day comes for his undoing and his downfall and his defeat.

What else are we to forget? *We are to learn how to forget our sorrows*—and sooner or later these sorrows come to us, each and all. We are to learn how to forget them. When the sorrows come, we are to learn how to take these sorrows to the great, refining, overruling Master and ask Him so to dispose, so to rule and over-rule in them and with them that we may come out of them all refined and disciplined, the better educated and more useful because of such sorrows. They tell us that when you break the oyster's shell at a certain place it will go somewhere into the deep and find a pearl and mend that broken place in its shell with a beautiful pearl. Even so, when your sorrow in life comes, you are to learn how to take that sorrow and so have it woven into the warp and woof of your life that you shall not be weaker and worse for the sorrow, but shall be richer and stronger and better because of such sorrow. Read every now and then the polished essay of Emerson, "Compensation." Running all through this world is that clear principle of compensation. The Bible recognizes it: "For our light affliction, which is but for a moment, worketh for us a far more exceeding and eternal weight of glory" (2 Cor. 4:17). We are to lay to heart that sublimest truth that "all things work together for good to them that love God" (Rom. 8:28). Yonder in the asylum for the deaf and dumb a visitor went one day, and the superintendent of the asylum said: "Let me show you how bright these little children are, even though they are deaf and dumb. Ask any question you will," said the superintendent to the visitor. "Write your question there on the board, and see the answers that these little mutes will give to your question." He asked question after question, did this visitor. After awhile he asked a cruel question. I wonder how he could have done it. He wrote this cruel question there on the board: "If God loved you, why did He make you deaf and dumb?" Then the little things bowed their shoulders and sobbed for a moment with almost uncontrollable emotion. Presently a little tiny girl came from out her seat there, and went to the blackboard and wrote under that question these wonderful words of Jesus: "Even so, Father; for so it seemed good in thy sight" (Matt. 11:26). Wasn't it glorious? You and I are to take our sorrows, our black Fridays, our lone and long nights, and we are to come to Him and say: "Manage thou these, thou wondrous Friend, who canst turn the very night into morning; manage these for me." And we are to sing with Whittier when he sang:

> I know not where His islands lift
> Their fronded palms in air;
> But this I know, I cannot drift
> Beyond His love and care.

What else are we to forget? *We are to learn how to forget our sins.* If Paul had not learned how to forget his sins he would have been crippled utterly, clear to his death. Paul consented to the death of Stephen. Paul persecuted the church. Paul was a ringleader in sin. Paul seemed to run the whole gamut of sin. He called himself the chief of sinners, and perhaps he was. If Paul had not learned how to forget those awful sins that mastered him back yonder, if he had not learned how to get past them, then he would have gone with accusing conscience and broken spirit clear to his grave. We shall have about us a ball and a chain and shall go groveling and despairing and defeated if we do not learn how to forget our sins. When we look at the debit side of our lives, do our hearts faint within us? Mine faints within me. But then the Master of life summons me and says: "Come over here and look at the credit side, and the credit side will outfigure all that debit side." And when I come over there I say to Him: "What dost thou mean, oh, thou gracious Friend?" Listen to Him, and He tells us: "Where sin abounded, grace did much more abound" (Rom. 5:20). Listen to Him again: "As far as the east is from the west, so far hath he removed our transgressions from us" (Ps. 103:12). And listen to Him yet again: "I have put your sins behind my back. I have drowned them in the depths of the sea. I will remember them against you no more forever" (see Isa. 38:17; Mic. 7;19; Jer. 31:34, my paraphrase). Oh, isn't that wonderful? Listen to Him again and He tells us: "The blood of Jesus Christ his Son cleanseth us from all sin" (1 John 1:7). When Satan comes with his accusing cry, reminding me of my weakness and my frailty and my transgressions and my proneness to sin and all that, he can make out his case, I grant it; but I come back and say to him, But, sir, where sin abounded, grace has much more abounded, and in Christ, whose name is Jesus, I have victory, even over my sins. "Thou shalt call his name Jesus: for he shall save his people from their sins" (Matt. 1:21). We have a real Savior from sin in Christ Jesus, and when we trust Him, no more are we to go hobbled, with ball and chain, because of sin, because Christ becomes our personal Savior from both the penalty and power of sin.

Years ago, in South Texas, there was a little home in the country burned down, and before the neighbors could rescue the family all were burned to death save one little girl, some nine or ten years of age, and she was badly burned on one side of her face and little body. The rest were all burned to death. The neighbors, after a few days, when they had consulted, sent little Mary to the far-famed Buckner Orphans' Home. They advised the noble head of that home when little Mary would come, on what train, and there good Dr. Buckner was waiting for her, of course. When she got off the train, her little eyes were red from weeping, and she seemed intuitively to know that he was her protector henceforth, and she started toward him saying: "Is this Mr. Buckner?" He said: "Yes, and is this little Mary?" And then she came and laid her little head up against his knee and sobbed with indescribable emotion and looked up at last with that little burned face and said: "You will have to be my papa and mamma both." He said: "I will, the best I can, Mary." And then she went into the home, and was looked after along with those hundreds of children.

I have been there time and again and preached to them. I have seen them come out to greet him when he would return to them after an absence. The little tots come down the avenue and vie with one another as they swing around him, each wishing to kiss him first. Along in that group one day came the little burned-faced Mary, and the little children kissed him as was their wont, but little Mary stood off several feet away, and looked across her shoulder watching the whole affair, sobbing like her heart would break. And when these little ones had kissed the good man, he looked across to her and said: "Mary, why don't you come and kiss me?" That was entirely too much for her and she sobbed aloud. Then he went over and touched her little chin and lifted it up and said: "I do not quite understand you, Mary. Why didn't you come to kiss me?" And the little thing had difficulty in speaking, and when she did speak she said: "O Papa Buckner, I could not ask you to kiss me, I am so ugly. After I got burned I am so ugly I could not ask you to kiss me, but if you will just love me like you love the other children and tell me you love me, then you need not kiss me at all." You know what he did. He pushed all those beautiful children away and took up little Mary in his arms and kissed the little burned cheek again and again and said: "Mary, you are just as beautiful to Papa Buckner as are any of the rest."

Ah, me! I was that burned child once, and sin did it all! I came to Jesus and said: "I am sorry. My heart is sick about it. Oh, I have repented of it all." And He said: "I will receive you, and I will give you the kiss of reconciliation, the kiss of pardon, the kiss of forgiveness," and I was saved when I came like that. Now no more will I go fettered and bound because of sin, because Christ has made me free by His mighty grace.

Jesus paid it all,
All to Him I owe,
Sin had left a crimson stain,
He washed it white as snow.

A Right Anticipation

Let me detain you for the third word. Paul had a right anticipation. "Forgetting those things which are behind, and reaching forth unto those things which are before, I press toward the mark for the prize of the high calling of God in Christ Jesus." Paul had a right forward look. My men and women, at this busy noonday hour, I come to ask you, one by one, have you the right aim in your life? What are you living for? What is that hand for? What is the eye for? What is human life for? What is your life for? How are you using your life? How are you investing your life? What is the aim of your life? Does somebody say: "Why, I am taking it one world at a time?" That is not bright. That is not clever. If a man does not include two worlds at a time, then he commits suicide for both. A man is to be a citizen of two worlds, and a man who lives simply for this world, no matter how successfully, how victoriously, how notoriously, if a man lives simply for this present world, he commits suicide in it and suicide for the world endless that awaits us just out there. Oh, include two worlds in your plan!

Let me tell you about three men. One said: "One world at a time for me," and from early morning until dewy eve, he invested all his powers to win success, and he won it. But he died without hope and without God, taking a leap into the dark with a wail, the memory of which must forever give agony to the hearts that heard it. The second one made profession of religion, but he followed Christ afar off. He put his religion into a little tiny corner of his life. He gave Jesus the small places, and when he came to the last end, with his family and minister around him, the minister was saddened by his awful story: "Sir, I trust I shall get to heaven, but my works are burned up because I have done little or nothing for Christ. Oh, if I could retrace my life and be the right kind of a man!" And then there was the third man. From life's young morning he dedicated his life to Jesus. He went his way a great businessman, but with it all he was the faithful friend of Jesus. He chose Christ as his chief partner, his guide in all things. And when he came down to die, there was a halo of light about his face, and there was victory in his heart and in his words, and all the men that knew him said: "If ever a Christian has lived, this man is he." Which one of these three men would you rather be? Listen to the words of a modern poet:

> I had walked life's way with an easy tread,
> Had followed where comforts and pleasures led,
> Until one day in a quiet place
> I met the Master face to face.

> With station and rank and wealth for my goal,
> Much thought for my body, but none for my soul,
> I had entered to win in life's mad race,
> When I met the Master face to face.

> I had built my castles and reared them high,
> With their towers had pierced the blue of the sky,
> I had sworn to rule with an iron mace,
> When I met the Master face to face.

> I met Him and knew Him and blushed to see
> That His eyes, full of sorrow, were fixed on me
> And I faltered and fell at His feet that day,
> While my castles melted and vanished away.

> Melted and vanished and in their place
> Naught else did I see but the Master's face,
> And I cried aloud, "Oh, make me meet
> To follow the steps of Thy wounded feet."

> My thought is now for the souls of men,
> I have lost my life to find it again,
> E'er since one day in a quiet place
> I met the Master face to face.

O my men and women, you are not ready to die, you are not ready to live, you are not ready for any duty even for five seconds if you are putting the wisdom and love and power of Christ out of your lives. Be wise, I summon you, and give heed to the supreme things, even in the day when you ought. That day is today.

NOTES

Paul the Ready

Charles Haddon Spurgeon (1834–1892) is undoubtedly the most famous minister of the nineteenth century. Converted in 1850, he united with the Baptists and soon began to preach in various places. He became pastor of the Baptist church in Waterbeach, England, in 1851, and three years later he was called to the decaying Park Street Church, London. Within a short time the work began to prosper, a new church was built and dedicated in 1861, and Spurgeon became London's most popular preacher. In 1855, he began to publish his sermons weekly; today they make up the fifty-seven volumes of *The Metropolitan Tabernacle Pulpit*. He founded a pastor's college and several orphanages.

This sermon is taken from *The Metropolitan Tabernacle Pulpit*, volume 38.

Charles Haddon Spurgeon

12

PAUL THE READY

I am ready (Romans 1:15).

I THINK PAUL MIGHT have used these words as his motto. We had once a Saxon king called Ethelred the Unready; here we have an apostle who might be called Paul the Ready. The Lord Jesus no sooner called to him out of heaven, "Saul, Saul, why persecutest thou me?" (Acts 9:4), than he answered, "Who art thou, Lord?" (v. 5) Almost directly after, his question was, "Lord, what wilt thou have me to do?" (v. 6). He was no sooner converted than he was ready for holy service; "straightway he preached Christ" (v. 20) in the synagogues at Damascus. All through his life, whatever happened to him, he was always ready. If he had to speak to crowds in the street, he had the fitting word; if to the elite upon Mars' hill, he was ready for the philosophers. If he talked to the Pharisees, he knew how to address them; when he was brought before the Sanhedrim and perceived the Pharisaic and Sadducean elements in it, he knew how to avail himself of their mutual jealousies to help his own escape. See him before Felix, before Festus, before Agrippa—he is always ready. When he came to stand before Nero, God was with him and delivered him out of the mouth of the lion. If you find him on board ship, he is ready to comfort men in the storm. When he gets on shore a shipwrecked prisoner, he is ready to gather sticks to help to make the fires. At all points he is an all-around man, and an all-ready man, always ready to go wherever his Master sends him and to do whatever his Lord appoints him.

In talking at this time about Paul's readiness, I shall, first, dwell for a little while upon the state of Paul's mind, as indicated by his declaration, "I am ready." Secondly, I shall show that this state of mind arose from excellent principles, and, thirdly, I shall point out that this readiness produces admirable results wherever it is to be found.

The State of Paul's Mind

I shall refer you to four passages where he expresses his readiness. The first is our text. Here we have *Paul's readiness to work*. "So, as much as in me is, I am ready to preach the gospel to you that are at Rome also." He had preached the Gospel throughout a great part of Asia, he had crossed over into Europe, he had proclaimed the Word through Greece; if ever an opportunity should occur for him to get to the capital of the world, whatever might be the danger to which he would be exposed, he was prepared to go. He was ready to go anywhere for Jesus, anywhere to preach the Gospel, anywhere to win a soul, anywhere to comfort the people of God. "I am ready." There is no place to which Paul was not ready to go. He was ready to make a journey into Spain, and if he did not come to this island of ours, which is a matter of question, undoubtedly he was ready to have gone to the utmost isles of the sea and to lands and rivers unknown to carry his Master's mighty Word. Are we as ready as Paul was to go anywhere for Jesus, or do we feel that we could only work for Christ at home and that we should not dare to go to the United States or to Australia or into some heathen land? Oh, may God keep us always on tiptoe ready to move if the cloud moves and equally ready to stay where we are if the cloud moves not!

If Paul went to Rome, he would be going into the lion's mouth, but he was ready for that, for lions had no kind of terror for him. He had fought with beasts at Ephesus. In spirit he had died in the mouth of the lion many a time, counting not his life dear to him. I wish we were ready for all danger, all slander, all contumely, all poverty, all or anything that it might cost us to preach Christ where He is not known. The apostle was ready to go anywhere with the Gospel, but he was not ready to preach another gospel. No one could make him ready to do that. He was not ready to hide the Gospel, he was not ready to tone it down, he was not ready to abridge it or to extend it. He said, "I am not ashamed of the gospel of Christ: for it is the power of God unto salvation to everyone that believeth; to the Jew first, and also to the Greek" (rom. 1:16). As to the matter of preaching the Gospel, Paul was always ready for that; he kept back not any one of its truths nor any part of its teaching. Even if it should bring upon him ridicule and contempt, though it should be to the Jews a stumbling block and to the Greeks foolishness, Paul would say, "As much as in me is, I am ready to preach the gospel" to them all. He did not always feel alike fit for the work; he did not always find the same openings or the same freedom in speech; but he was always ready to preach wherever the Lord gave him the opportunity.

If you will kindly turn to Acts 21:13, you will read, in the second place, of *Paul's readiness to suffer*. He says, "I am ready not to be bound only, but also to die at Jerusalem for the name of the Lord Jesus." This is perhaps a greater thing than the former one; to be ready to suffer is more than to be ready to serve. To some of us it has become a habit to be ready to preach the Gospel, but here was a man who was ready to suffer for the name of the Lord Jesus, so ready that he could not be dissuaded from it. He might preach the Gospel, but why must he go to Jerusalem? All the world was before him; why must he go to that persecuting city? Everybody told him that he would have bonds and imprisonment and perhaps death, but he cared nothing about all that. He said, "I am ready, I am ready."

Beloved friends, are we ready to be scoffed at, to be thought idiots, to be put down among old-fashioned fossils? Perhaps so. Are we ready, if we should be required to do so, to lose friends for Christ's sake, to have the cold shoulder for Christ's sake? Perhaps so.

Are we also ready, if it be the Lord's will, to go home, to be carried upstairs, and to lie there for the next three months? Are we as ready as that poor woman who said, "The Lord said to me, 'Betty, mind the house, look after the children,' and I did it. By and by, he said, 'Betty, go upstairs, and cough twelve months.' Shall I not do that also and not complain, for it is all that I can do?" "I am ready." You remember what is on the seal of the American Baptist Missionary Society, an ox with a plow on one side and a halter on the other, ready for either, ready to serve or ready to suffer. You have not come to the highest style of readiness until you are ready for whatever the will of God may appoint for you. Unreadiness from this point of view is very common, but it shows unsubdued human nature. It is a relic of rebellion, for when we are fully sanctified, when every thought is brought into subjection to the mind of God, then the cry is not, "As I will," but "As thou wilt."

Ah! dear friends, while I am talking very feebly to you, I should not wonder but what you are saying to yourselves, "This is above us as yet. We shall need much more teaching of the Holy Spirit before we are ready for unknown sufferings, for lonely sufferings, for suffering that seems to have no good in it, useless suffering, for being put on the shelf, for being laid aside from the holy services of God's house and from the little works that once we were able to do for Christ." Are you ready? Can you answer, "Ready, aye, ready"? So it should be with you if you belong to Christ, and so it was with Paul.

The third passage I must now quote is not exactly the same in words, but it means the same as the others. It tells us of Paul's readiness to do unpleasant work. I am afraid many of God's servants fall short here. The passage is in 2 Corinthians 10:6: "And having in a readiness to revenge all disobedience, when your obedience is fulfilled." The church at Corinth had sunk into a very sad condition. It was a church that did not have any minister; it had an open ministry, and nobody knows what mischief comes of that kind of thing. Paul recommended them to try what a minister could do for them, for he said, "I beseech you, brethren, (ye know the house of Stephanas, that it is the firstfruits of Achaia, and that they have addicted themselves to the ministry of the saints,) that you submit yourselves unto such." They were too gifted for that, and everybody wanted to speak. When a church is all mouth, what becomes of the body? If it were all mouth, it would simply become a vacuum, nothing more, and the church in Corinth became very much that. It was nobody's business to administer discipline, for it was everybody's business. What is everybody's business is nobody's business, as we well know, so no discipline was administered, and the church became what we call "all sixes and sevens." It stands in the Scriptures forever as a warning against that method of church government, or, rather, of no church government at all.

Paul, when he went among these people, determined to administer discipline and to try to put things right. He was not going to Corinth with a sword or with any carnal weapon or with anything of unkindness or hasty temper, but he was going with the Word of God. He wrote, "The weapons of our warfare are not carnal, but mighty through God to the pulling down of strong holds" (2 Cor. 10:4). He meant to go among the Corinthian professors and pull down the stronghold of heathen vice that had entered the church to such an extent that even at the Lord's Table some of them were drunken. Paul meant to deal honestly with all who were dishonoring the name of Christ. Now, dear friends, I speak especially to brethren whom God has put into the ministry or put into office in the church, are you ready for this unpleasant duty? Oh, it costs some of us a great deal to say a strong thing! Perhaps we cannot say it at all without getting into a temper, and then we had better not say it at all. It is not easy to have firmness in the language combined with sweetness in the manner of uttering it. It is easy to congratulate friends, it is not difficult to condemn them in the gross. But it is another thing to speak personally and faithfully to each erring one and to be assured in our own souls that, as far as we have any responsibility in the matter, we will not tolerate an Achan in the camp and will not have evil done knowingly in the house of God. It should be our endeavor, as God has made us overseers, not to overlook things that are evil, but really to oversee everything that is committed to our charge and to try to set right whatever is wrong.

Is it not the case with you who are private members of churches, do you not sometimes find it difficult to rebuke sin? Even profane swearing will come under the notice of many Christian people without a word of rebuke from them. They say they thought it best to hold their tongues; you mean you thought it easiest for yourselves. Sometimes known wickedness comes before the eyes of Christians, and they excuse themselves and say, "We did not like to interfere." "Perhaps they were too gentle," you say; I suggest that they were too lazy, too much inclined to save their own precious skins, too anxious to have the soft side of this life, and not willing to endure hardness as good soldiers of Jesus Christ. Are you ready, as Paul was, to exhibit a holy indignation against sin and lovingly and tenderly, yet firmly, in the name of the Lord to see that evil does not go unrebuked? If any man has come to this, I will not say that I envy him, but that I desire to be found in that position, so that, when the Lord comes none of the evil of this generation may lie at my door. When He shall come and find His church lukewarm, faithless, adulterated by worldliness and all manner of heresies, I pray that He may not have to point His finger at unfaithful pastors and say of any one of us, "Thou art the man who art responsible for this sad state of affairs." Oh, may God make us ready for whatever is laid upon us; however unpleasant and contrary to our mind and feeling the task may be, may we be ready to do the Lord's work, faithful even to the end!

Now, once more, will you kindly turn to 2 Timothy 4:6, where you have a verse well known to you all, "For I am now ready to be offered, and the time of my departure is at hand." *Paul was ready to die*; he was ready to loose his cable from earth and to sail away to the haven of the blessed. Well he might be, for he could add, "I have fought a good fight, I have finished my course, I have kept the faith: henceforth there is laid up for me a crown of righteousness, which the Lord, the righteous judge, shall give me at that day: and not to me only, but unto all them also that love his appearing" (vv. 7–8). Beloved friends, we cannot be ready to die unless we have been taught how to live. We who are active and have talents to use and health and strength with which to use those talents must go on with "the greatest fight in the world" until we can say, "I have fought a good fight." We must go on running the Christian race until we can say, "I have finished my course." We must go on guarding the Word of God and holding fast the truth of God until we can say, "I have kept the faith." It will be hard work to lie dying if we have been unfaithful. God's infinite mercy may come in and forgive and help us, and we may be saved, yet so as by fire (see 1 Cor. 3:15). But if we would look forward to death with perfect readiness, having no dread or fear about it, but being as ready to die as we are to go to our beds tonight, then we must be kept faithful to God by His almighty grace. The faith must keep us, and we must keep the faith.

Thus, you see, Paul was ready for service, ready for suffering, ready for unpleasant duty, and ready to die. If I were to go around this tabernacle and ask of everyone, "My friend, are you ready in these four ways?" how many of you would be able to answer, "We are ready"? I am afraid many would have to shake their heads and say, "I do not know what to say; I am doing my best in some style, but I cannot say that I have the readiness that the apostle claimed."

Paul's Readiness Arose
from Excellent Principles

As for Paul's readiness to preach, I should trace that to *his solemn conviction of the truth of the Gospel*. If a man only thinks it is true he will not care whether he preaches it or does not preach it, but if he knows it is true, then he must preach it. I do not think we need find much fault with people nowadays for being too positive and dogmatic about the truth of God; the present current runs in quite another direction. A feeble faith, which might almost be mistaken for unbelief, is the common thing, and hence there is no great readiness to speak. Paul wrote to the Corinthians, "As it is written, I believed, and therefore have I spoken; we also believe, and therefore speak" (2 Cor. 4:13). If I get a grip of a thing and know it is true, then I must tell it to others. The backbone of the preaching of Christ is a conviction of the truth of Christ.

Paul also had a dauntless courage in this matter. He said, "Woe is unto me, if I preach not the gospel!" (1 Cor. 9:16). Whatever happened to him if he did preach it, he had counted the cost, and he was quite ready for all the consequences of his action. He had a holy self-denial, so that he put himself out of the question. "I am ready for anything; I am ready to preach this gospel, if I am stoned, if I am thrown cut of the city as dead, if I am imprisoned, if I am sent into the den of Caesar at Rome." Paul was ready because his courage had been given him of God.

Paul was ready to preach the Gospel at Rome because *he had freed himself from all entanglement*. You know how he put it in writing to his son Timothy, "No man that warreth entangleth himself with the affairs of this life; that he may please him who hath chosen him to be a soldier" (2 Tim. 2:4). There are some of us who get so tied up and entangled that we are not ready to do God's service because we are all in knots through too much worldly business. Try, dear friends, you who are the servants of Christ, to keep yourselves as clear as you can of all entanglements. You have your living to earn, but serve God while you are earning it. If you see an opportunity of getting rich, but in order to do so you will have to deny yourself from Christ's work, you will have to give up weeknight services, and so on, do not thus entangle yourself. Keep yourself as clear us you can. Her Majesty does not expect one of her soldiers to take to farming and then to send word that he cannot go to battle because he has to get in his hay harvest or he has his wheat to cut. He must come whenever he is called, and blessed is that good soldier of Jesus Christ who can come when he is wanted by his King and Captain. Sir Colin Campbell, when told that he was wanted to go to India, was asked, "How long will you take to get ready, Sir Colin?" He replied, "Twenty-four hours"; in twenty-four hours he was ready to go. A Moravian was about to be sent by Zinzendorf to preach in Greenland. He had never heard of it before. But his leader called him and said, "Brother, will you go to Greenland?" He answered, "Yes, sir." "When will you go?" "When my boots come home from the cobbler." And he did go as soon as his boots came home. He wanted nothing else but just that pair of boots, and he was ready to go. Paul, not even waiting for his boots to come home from the cobbler, says, "I am ready." Oh, it is grand to find a man so little entangled that he can go where God would have him go and can go at once.

Paul had, besides, such love for men, whether they were Jews or Romans or any other people, that he was ready to go anywhere to save them. He had also *such zeal for God* that it was a happiness to him to think of going to the furthest region if he might but preach Christ where He was not known, not building on another man's foundation, but laying the first stone of the edifice himself. This, then, accounted for his readiness to preach: a holy conviction of the truth of what he had to preach and of the need of preaching it.

But what helped Paul to be ready to suffer? Some here will have to suffer for Jesus Christ's sake, though they may never be called to preach. Well, I should say, dear friends, first, that *Paul was completely consecrated to the Lord*. He was not his own, he was bought with a price, and that led him to feel that his Master might do whatever He liked with him. He belonged to Christ, he was Jesus Christ's branded slave, and he was absolutely at Christ's disposal. Moreover, *he had such trust in his Lord* that he felt, whatever He does with me, it will be good and kind, and therefore I will make no condition, I will have no reserve from Him; it is the Lord, let Him do what seemeth Him good." He had resolved to serve his Lord; therefore, if he had to be bound or to die, he would not shrink back. He could have sung, as we sometimes sing, but he could carry it out better than we do—

> Through floods and flames, if Jesus lead,
> I'll follow where he goes.

A wholehearted consecration, a childlike confidence, a deep-toned submission—these will make us ready for suffering, whatever it may be.

But however did Paul screw himself up to be ready to exercise discipline? That is, to me, the ugliest point of all. How could he bring himself to be able to do that? I think it was because *he had not received his gospel of men*, nor by men, and he had learned not to depend upon men nor to look for their approval as the support of his life. He was able to lean on the Savior and to walk alone with his Lord. So long as he had Christ with him, he wanted nobody else. *Paul had learned the fear of God which casts out the fear of man.* "Who art thou, that thou shouldest be afraid of a man that shall die, and of the son of man which shall be made as grass; and forgettest the LORD thy maker?" (Isa. 51:12–13). Remembering man leads to the forgetting of God. If we learn to speak very plainly, yet very lovingly, habitually cultivating frankness toward all Christian people and even toward the ungodly and do not know what it is to ask of any man leave to speak the truth, how much better it will be all around! May the Holy Spirit deepen in us the fear of God and so take away from us the fear of man!

Then, with Paul, each of us will be ready to say, even concerning the most unpleasant duty, "I am ready."

But how came he to be able to say that he was ready to die? I will not dwell upon that. I have already told you that he felt ready to die because he could say that, as far as he had gone, *he had finished the work God gave him to do, and he had kept the faith*. Ah, dear friends, it is nothing but keeping faithful to God that will enable you to treat death as a friend! One dereliction of duty will be sufficient to rob you of comfort. When a traveler is walking, a very small stone in his shoe will lame him; a very small offense against the integrity that God requires of His servants may do us great mischief. Did you ever notice in Gideon's life that he had seventy sons, his own legitimate sons, and that he had one son who was the child of a harlot, and that one, Abimelech, killed his father's seventy sons? So it may be that a good man has seventy virtues, but if he tolerates one wrong thing, it will be enough to rob him of the comfort of all the good things of this life, so that, when he comes to die, he may go limping and lame. Aye, and all his life long, he may go, like David did, halting even to the grave. May the Lord in mercy and love keep us right! If He teaches us how to live, we shall know how to die.

It is not dying that is the great difficulty, it is living. If we are but helped to fight the good fight of faith, to finish our course, and to keep the faith, we shall die right enough. As Mr. Wesley said when the good woman asked him, "Do you not sometimes feel an awe at the thought of dying?" "No," he replied, "If I knew for certain that I was going to die tomorrow night, I should do just exactly what I am going to do. I am going to preach [I think it was] at Gloucester this afternoon, and this evening; and I shall go to lodge with friend So-and-so. I shall stay up with him until ten o'clock, and then I shall go to bed. I shall be up at five and ride over to Tewkesbury, and I shall preach there and shall go to friend So-and-so's for the night. I shall go to bed at ten o'clock; and whether I live or not, it does not matter at all to me, for if I die, I shall wake up in glory. That is what I am going to do, whether I live or die." It was said of Mr. Whitefield that he never went to bed at night leaving even a pair of gloves out of its place; he used to say that he would like to have everything ready in case he might be taken away. I think I see that good man standing, with a bedroom candle in his hand, at the top of the staircase preaching Christ the last night of his life to the people sitting on the stairs, then going inside the room and commending himself to God, and going straight away to heaven. That is the way to die, but if you do not live like Wesley and Whitefield lived, you cannot die like Wesley and Whitefield died. No, God grant us grace that we may be perfectly ready to die when the time for our departure is at hand!

This Readiness Produces Admirable Results

First, *it prevents surprise*. It is always bad to be taken by surprise. He who lives to the Lord shall not fear evil tidings, for his heart is fixed, trusting in the Lord. If you are perfectly submissive to God's will, and, as you crossed your threshold tonight, you heard that your child was dead or that your dearest friend was smitten with sore sickness, you would say, "Well, I stoop to the surrender. When I had my children, I did not think they were immortal. I knew they would die, and I have stood ready for anything that might happen to them." Oh, brethren, it is because we are not submissive, not sanctified, not fully resigned to God's will that we get tripped up every now and then and do not quite know where we are! May the Lord give us the grace to be prepared for every emergency!

Again, when a man is ready, *it prevents loss of time and opportunity*. Many a sportsman has lost his bird because he was not ready to take aim; many a fisherman has lost his fish because he has not been ready to grasp his rod and put the line into the stream. Many a preacher has, no doubt, missed the mark because, when he might have said a word for Christ, he was not ready to say it. Have you not often gone home and said to yourself, "Now I recollect what I ought to have said. That man made an observation, and I could not tell at the moment what to reply to it. I know now what I should have said"? It is a fine thing to be wise when it is too late, but it would be much better if we waited upon God and asked Him to make us ready, ever ready, to speak for Him in every place and at any time, whenever an opportunity occurs.

Readiness also helps us *to make good use of every occasion*. He who is ready as each occasion comes not only snatches the first part of it, but all the rest of it; he is prepared to deal with the whole thing as it proceeds. He who is always doing his Master's work learns how to do it well, but he who only does it occasionally is like a bad workman who half forgets his craft because he is so much engaged in doing something else. God keep us all ready! No, you be ready tonight to say a good word to somebody on your way home and to serve God in your family when you get home!

To be ready *puts a bloom on obedience* and presents it to God at its best. Some Sunday school children were once asked what was the meaning of doing the will of God on earth as it is done in heaven, and they gave some very pretty answers. One said, "In heaven they do God's will always." Another said, "They do God's will cheerfully." But one said, "Please, sir, they do God's will directly." That is the thing; that is how it is done in heaven, directly. May we be in such a state of heart that we are ready to do the Lord's will directly!

In this readiness our *obedience is multiplied*. I mean that any one act is multiplied, for the man who is ready to do the right thing has already done it in the sight of God. The Lord accepts it as done, and then, if the man still remains ready, he does, as it were, do the thing again, and when it is actually done he is still ready to do it again. If the act is only one, yet to God's eye it has a teeming multitude of obedient actions swarming around it.

To be ready, especially to be ready to die, *removes all fear of death.* I wish we could all sing as she did who died in her sleep and left this verse written on a piece of paper by her bedside—

> Since Jesus is mine, I'll not fear undressing,
> But gladly put off these garments of clay;
> To die in the Lord, is a covenant blessing,
> Since Jesus to glory through death led the way.

If we are ready as Paul was, all fear of death will be gone from us.

And I think it *takes away a thousand ills* if we are ready for service, ready for suffering, ready to die. I will tell you one thing, dear sister over yonder, you would not be so ready to halt as you are if you were ready for the Lord's work and the Lord's will. And you who are ready to perish would get out of that sad kind of readiness if you came and trusted Christ and became ready to suffer or to do the Master's will. The Lord is ready to pardon; may we be ready to believe. And may we come at once to Him, accept salvation through Jesus Christ, and then all through the rest of our lives say to the great Captain of our salvation what good sailors reply to their captain's call, "Ready, aye ready! Ready for storms and ready for calms; ready for whatever Thou dost command, ready for whatever Thou dost ordain!" The Lord bless you, dear friends, and give all of you this readiness, for Christ's sake! Amen.

Additional Sermon Resources

Great Women of the Bible   Clarence E. Macartney
A collection of sermons from a master pulpiteer of yesterday. Macartney's unique descriptive style brings these women of the Bible to life and provides inspirational reading for all Christians.

ISBN 0-8254-3268-5   **208 pp.**   **paperback**

The Greatest Questions of the Bible and of Life   Clarence E. Macartney
Discussing such questions as What shall I do with Jesus? What must I do to be saved? If a man dies, shall he live again? and Barabbas or Jesus? Clarence E. Macartney challenges his readers to ask questions and seek the answers from the pages of Holy Scripture and employ this method of teaching in his or her own situation to great profit.

ISBN 0-8254-3273-1   **192 pp.**   **paperback**

Greatest Texts of the Bible   Clarence E. Macartney
This collection of sermons represents some of the author's strongest and most impassioned preaching. Except for slight modifications and updating, and the insertion of Scripture references where needed, these sermons are reissued in their original form.

ISBN 0-8254-3266-9   **208 pp.**   **paperback**

The Greatest Words in the Bible and in Human Speech   Clarence E. Macartney
A group of fifteen sermons based on fifteen words from men's speech and their corresponding biblical meaning and significance. Macartney explores such words as: sin, forgiveness, now, whisperer, tomorrow, why, repent, heaven, memory, prayer, death, and experience.

ISBN 0-8254-3271-5   **192 pp.**   **paperback**

He Chose Twelve   Clarence E. Macartney
This careful study of the New Testament illuminates the personality and individuality of each of the Twelve Disciples. A carefully crafted series of Bible character sketches including chapters on all the apostles as well as Paul and John the Baptist.

ISBN 0-8254-3270-7   **176 pp.**   **paperback**

Paul the Man   Clarence E. Macartney
Macartney delves deeply into Paul's background and heritage, helping twentieth-century Christians understand what made him the pivotal figure of New Testament history. Paul, the missionary and theologian, are carefully traced in this insightful work.

ISBN 0-8254-3269-3   **208 pp.**   **paperback**

Twelve Great Questions About Christ   Clarence E. Macartney
Macartney addresses commonly asked questions about the life and person of Jesus Christ. The integrity of the Scriptures underlies the provocative answers that Dr. Macartney provides in this thoughtful book. The broad range of subject matter will inform and inspire laymen and clergy alike as they peruse these pages.

ISBN 0-8254-3267-7   **160 pp.**   **paperback**

Treasury of the World's Great Sermons   **Warren W. Wiersbe**
These outstanding sermons are presented from 122 of the greatest preachers. A short biographical sketch of every preacher is also included. Complete with an index of texts and sermons.

ISBN 0-8254-4002-5   **672 double-column pp.**   **paperback**

Classic Sermons on the Attributes of God   **Warren W. Wiersbe**
These classic sermons lay a solid foundation for the study of God's attributes such as truth, holiness, sovereignty, omnipresence, immutability, and love. Includes messages by Henry Ward Beecher, J. D. Jones, J. H. Jowett, D. L. Moody, and John Wesley.

ISBN 0-8254-4038-6   **160 pp.**   **paperback**

Classic Sermons on the Birth of Christ   **Warren W. Wiersbe**
The central theme of the Bible is expanded and expounded in this collection of sermons from such great preachers as Henry P. Liddon, Walter A. Maier, G. Campbell Morgan, Arthur T. Pierson, and James S. Stewart.

ISBN 0-8254-4044-0   **160 pp.**   **paperback**

Classic Sermons on Christian Service   **Warren W. Wiersbe**
Dynamic principles for Christian service will be found in these classic sermons by highly acclaimed pulpit masters. Warren W. Wiersbe has carefully selected sermons which describe the essential characteristics of Christian servanthood.

ISBN 0-8254-4041-6   **160 pp.**   **paperback**

Classic Sermons on the Cross of Christ   **Warren W. Wiersbe**
An inspiring collection of sermons on perhaps the most significant event the world ever experienced—the cross of Christ. Through masterful sermons by great pulpit masters, the reader will gain a greater understanding of the theological, devotional, and practical importance of the cross of Christ.

ISBN 0-8254-4040-8   **160 pp.**   **paperback**

Classic Sermons on Faith and Doubt   **Warren W. Wiersbe**
A collection of 12 carefully selected sermons, the goal of which is to stimulate the growth and maturity of the believer's faith. Among the preachers represented are A. C. Dixon, J. H. Jowett, D. Martyn Lloyd-Jones, G. Campbell Morgan, and Martin Luther.

ISBN 0-8254-4028-9   **160 pp.**   **paperback**

Classic Sermons on Family and Home   **Warren W. Wiersbe**
The erosion of traditional family and biblical values is accelerating at an alarming rate. Dr. Wiersbe has compiled *Classic Sermons on Family and Home* to help recapture God's enduring truth for the family today.

ISBN 0-8254-4054-8   **160 pp.**   **paperback**

Classic Sermons on Hope   **Warren W. Wiersbe**
Crime. Poverty. Disease. War. Social upheaval. Ecological disaster. Warren W. Wiersbe has chosen twelve classic sermons on hope that will encourage the reader to face struggles with a confident Christian hope. Included are sermons by G. Campbell Morgan, D. L. Moody, Charles Spurgeon, and A. W. Tozer. Excellent starter material for sermon preparation; solid spiritual content for devotional readers.

ISBN 0-8254-4045-9   **160 pp.**   **paperback**

Classic Sermons on the Names of God   **Warren W. Wiersbe**
Any study of the names of God in Scripture will be enhanced by the classic sermons
included in this collection. They feature sermons from Charles H. Spurgeon, G.
Campbell Morgan, John Ker, George Morrison, Alexander MacLaren, and George
Whitefield.

ISBN 0-8254-4052-1   **160 pp.**   **paperback**

Classic Sermons on Overcoming Fear   **Warren W. Wiersbe**
Classic sermons by such famous preachers as Alexander Maclaren, V. Raymond
Edman, Clarence Macartney, George H. Morrison, Charles H. Spurgeon, George W.
Truett and others. Wiersbe has chosen sermons which offer insight as well as hope
for believers faced with the uncertainty of this pilgrim journey.

ISBN 0-8254-4043-2   **160 pp.**   **paperback**

Classic Sermons on Prayer   **Warren W. Wiersbe**
Fourteen pulpit giants present the need for and the results of a life permeated with
prayer. These sermons by such famous preachers as Dwight L. Moody, G. Campbell
Morgan, Charles H. Spurgeon, Reuben A. Torrey, Alexander Whyte, and others, will
help you experience the strength and power of God in prayer.

ISBN 0-8254-4029-7   **160 pp.**   **paperback**

Classic Sermons on the Prodigal Son   **Warren W. Wiersbe**
These sermons by highly acclaimed pulpit masters offer unique insights into perhaps
the most famous of Christ's parables. These sermons will provide new understanding
of the relationships between the son, father and other son. Believers will also be
challenged to apply the wonderful truth of the Father's love to their own lives.

ISBN 0-8254-4039-4   **160 pp.**   **paperback**

Classic Sermons on the Resurrection of Christ   **Warren W. Wiersbe**
These sermons represent the best in scholarship, warmed by deep inspiration and
enlivened by excitement about what the Resurrection of Christ means to the believer.

ISBN 0-8254-4042-4   **160 pp.**   **paperback**

Classic Sermons on the Second Coming and
Other Prophetic Themes   **Warren W. Wiersbe**
The second coming of Christ is a promise presented in many New Testament passages.
Dr. Wiersbe has marshaled an array of classic sermons on Christ's coming by great
preachers such as C. H. Spurgeon, G. Campbell Morgan, C. E. Macartney, and
Alexander MacLaren.

ISBN 0-8254-4051-3   **160 pp.**   **paperback**

Classic Sermons on the Sovereignty of God   **Warren W. Wiersbe**
Sovereignty. All authority, power, dominion, and majesty belong to God. Warren W.
Wiersbe has chosen twelve classic sermons that capture the glory and grace of this
divine attribute. Included are sermons by Paul Little, R. A. Torrey, C. H. Spurgeon,
and Jonathon Edwards. Excellent starter material for sermon preparation; solid spiritual
content for devotional readers.

0-8254-4055-6   **160 pp.**   **paperback**

Classic Sermons on Spiritual Warfare   **Warren W. Wiersbe**
In a timely new compilation of classic sermons, Dr. Warren Wiersbe offers eleven
expositions dealing with various facets of Satanic activity. Included are sermons by

such outstanding preachers as William Culbertson, Allan Redpath, D. Martyn Lloyd-Jones, G. Campbell Morgan, and C. H. Spurgeon.

ISBN 0-8254-4049-1   **160 pp.**   **paperback**

Classic Sermons on Suffering   **Warren W. Wiersbe**
Sermons by such illustrious preachers as C.H. Spurgeon, Phillips Brooks, John Calvin, Walter A. Maier, George W. Truett, and others that will uplift the depressed, comfort the heartbroken, and be especially useful for the preacher in his pulpit and counseling ministries.

ISBN 0-8254-4027-0   **204 pp.**   **paperback**

Classic Sermons on Worship   **Warren W. Wiersbe**
In these classic sermons by pulpiteers such as C. H. Spurgeon, John A. Broadus, James S. Stewart, Frederick W. Robertson, G. Campbell Morgan, and Andrew A. Bonar, we discover the true meaning of worship and are challenged to practice it.

ISBN 0-8254-4037-8   **160 pp.**   **paperback**